DAVID SABOL

WITH KAM GHAFFARI

Wood Carving
Basics

The Taunton Press

The Taunton Press
Inspiration for hands-on living®

The Taunton Press, Inc., 63 South Main Street, PO Box 5506, Newtown, CT 06470-5506
e-mail: tp@taunton.com

Editors: Marty Miller, Kam Ghaffari
Copy editor: Tammalene Mitman
Indexer: James Curtis
Jacket/Cover design: Kimberly Adis
Interior design: Kimberly Adis
Layout: Susan Lampe-Wilson
Illustrators: John Hartman and Christine Erikson
Photographer: Gary Junken & Scott Phillips

Library of Congress Cataloging-in-Publication Data
Sabol, David.
  Wood carving basics / David Sabol.
     p. cm.
  ISBN 978-1-56158-888-6
  1. Wood-carving. I. Title.
  TT199.7.S2128 2008
  731.4'62--dc22

                       2007030236

Printed in China
10 9 8 7 6 5 4

ACKNOWLEDGMENTS

NOT MANY PEOPLE GET TO SPEND THEIR LIVES DOING something they enjoy. I was lucky, but I have not pursued this love of mine entirely unassisted. I wish to thank the thousands of people I've met in the carving world over these many years—fellow carvers, students, and other artists—whose genuine friendship, enthusiasm, and support have allowed me to continue in my career.

Special smiles go to Helen Albert, who first asked me to do this book and DVD project. She always was there to calm my frequent panic attacks. My deepest gratitude, also, goes to Niki Palmer, whose steady voice on the phone helped make me meet deadlines I had thought were impossible, and to my videographer, Gary Junken, whose humor made having a video camera in my face for ten hours a day every day very enjoyable.

Special thanks to all the Taunton people—editors, copy editors, designers, and photographers (especially Randy O'Rourke, from whom I learned so much), and staff of the marketing department. Also, to Marty Miller, who edited my words so that even I can understand them.

A very special thank you goes to my wife, Laura, for all the big and even bigger things you did for me and this project.

Finally, a big kiss to my son and daughter, Kyle and Jessie. You are the finest work of art I've ever had a hand in. I'm so proud of both of you!

Contents

live your dream

INTRODUCTION

I'VE BEEN A WOOD-CARVER ALL MY LIFE, and have never had a job other than carving. I started when I was 8 years old with a pocketknife I pocketed from my grandmother's attic. I tried sharpening it on a stone birdbath in her backyard and slit my thumb open. A sharp knife, my first cut, and I was hooked!

My grandfather was a blade sharpener for the Remington® Arms Company. My father gave me the old Remington knife I still have and taught me how to carve wooden ship models and balsa-wood airplanes. After a while, I tired of following other people's blueprints and started creating my own small animals and birds.

I began haunting flea markets and garage sales, looking for tools, boxes—anything to do with wood carving. I gradually expanded my practice work into larger birds and decoys, little flower pins, and Christmas ornaments. I started selling my work at local churches and village-green shows.

I turned my bedroom into a carving studio and began to devote all my time outside of school to my passion. Going to one show after another, I became close friends with all the other exhibitors. It was an enjoyable way to spend my youth.

When I graduated from college in 1983, I had already been around the show circuits, and I knew all the promoters and venues; it just seemed natural to pursue carving as a career and see where it might lead. It has been my full-time occupation ever since.

I've had many incarnations: I was a sign carver for a number of years, doing all kinds of wooden signs for businesses and historical sites. When bird carving reached a peak of popularity in the '80s, I gravitated to carving birds and spent about 10 years doing that. I learned to carve efficiently, and developed a lot of techniques for carving birds out of single pieces of wet wood (rather than gluing on feathers and wings and heads). I then moved into doing caricatures and when my son was born in 1990, started doing the storybook characters that some of you may have seen.

I guess throughout my life I wasn't interested in being categorized as a certain style of carver; I didn't want to be known as a duck carver or a caricature carver. I have a voracious interest in and love for it all—everything from relief carvings to figures to wildlife, signs, gunstocks, table legs—anything that would come along, I would say, "Yeah, I can do that," and I did it.

Over the years I have developed a vast background in all styles and disciplines of carving. That is why I was really excited about this book and DVD project—through it I'm able to share my love of wood carving with others. The simple enjoyment of being able to relax, take a piece of wood and a knife, and create something with your very own hands is a rare pleasure in our frenzied culture.

I've put together a sampler of a broad variety of avenues that are open to you as you learn to carve. The projects are geared toward the beginner, but as you progress through the book, you'll gain the valuable skills and techniques you'll need to grow as a carver, experimenting with your own pieces. Every piece you do will hone your skills for the projects that follow. After a while, you'll gain the confidence to try things that you may have been hesitant to attempt at first.

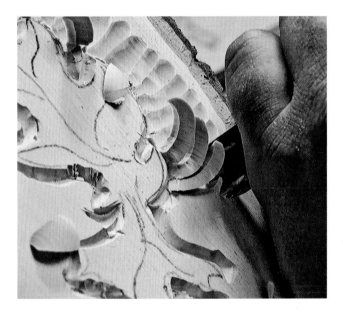

Everything takes practice. I consider all of the pieces I've done throughout my life as practice pieces. Be open to letting pieces evolve as you work on them. Take things in this book a little further, or simplify them. Deviate from the design; let things happen. Sometimes spontaneity is the best inspiration—I get some of my best pieces out of things that started off as one idea and grew into something completely different.

If I were asked to list the three most important elements in carving, I'd say the first is an idea, the inspiration—what you want to carve. The second is a piece of wood; again, there are many choices. The third element is a sharp carving tool. Many people become frustrated when they begin carving because they feel they don't have the ability, when, in fact, their tools are not allowing them to create what they want to create. I have provided an in-depth section on sharpening to make sure your creativity isn't hampered by the lack of this easily learned skill.

Carving is a personal expression, a simple art form that goes back thousands of years. It's something you can share with your children and grandchildren. People always enjoy a handmade gift, something you took the time to create for them. And that's what this is all about—to help you create what you see in your mind and your heart. I hope you come to enjoy wood carving as much as I do.

I remember a 7th-grade biology teacher had a sticker on his door that said, "Free knowledge; bring your own container." Well here's the knowledge. Keep it fresh and use it often; you've got your own container.

Tools and Woods

CARVING, LIKE MANY hobbies and professions, involves a tremendous variety of tools and materials. There are pocketknives, specialty knives, chisels, gouges, V-tools, and many other pieces of equipment and accessories. And once you get past the tools (which you may never completely do), you'll find a host of material and finishing choices waiting for you. If you're just beginning, the array may seem daunting. But trust your affinity for this expressive hobby to carry you through.

Tools are the lifeblood of any trade, yet with all these gadgets competing for your hard-earned dollar, the question is: What do you really need to get started? There's no magic tool to help you create miraculous work. However, wise shopping decisions can make your carving projects easier and more enjoyable. If you purchase the best quality possible (and that doesn't necessarily mean the most expensive), you will benefit as a carver in the long run.

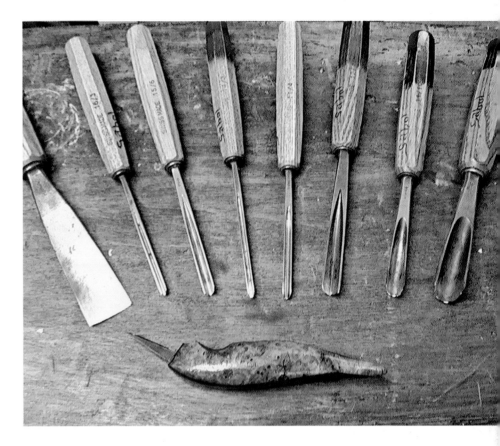

BASIC STARTER TOOL SET
These tools represent the basic collection you need to get started. You'll do 90 percent of your carving with this set (left to right): 2/30 gouge, 16/3 V-tool, 15/6 V-tool, 11/3 and 11/4 gouges, 12/10 V-tool, 11/10 gouge, and 11/15 gouge; (below): detail knife.

IN THE COURSE OF THE 38 OR SO YEARS

I've been carving, I've collected a vast array of tools. In fact, like most carvers, I have a sickness for collecting tools. I love tools. If there is a new one, I have to have it. Whether or not I'm actually going to use that tool is another question entirely.

That said, you really don't need an entourage of equipment for carving. For the majority of my work, I use only a handful of tools. The fewer tools you own, the fewer you have to sharpen and carry around with you, and the less time you'll spend worrying about which tool to use for a given situation. You learn to be efficient with what you have. You get familiar with what your tools will do, and you find different ways to apply them, so you can use them in various situations where you might have thought you should have another tool.

I've assembled a small assortment of the basic tools that I use for about 90 percent of my carving (see the photo above). These make a good starter set, which you can add to progressively as you see the need. Though I occasionally use a few other gouges in the projects I'll show you, the starter set contains all the tools I suggest my students bring to class, and you can do any of the projects in this book with this core collection.

Then there's the question of what woods to use. Not every species, of course, makes a good carving medium, so it's probably wise to limit your choices to the few discussed in this chapter when you're starting out. But even among these specialized species, each has its own distinctive feel under your knife or cutting tool. And aspects natural to wood itself, such as grain direction, growth rings, and moisture content, will affect the way the wood works and how precisely it holds the details of your design.

Thus, even if you select a suitable species, you may not have control over what nature has produced, but you do have wide choices when it comes to matching the specific piece of wood to the project at hand.

If you live close to a sawmill, you might find it best to buy your carving stock there. If there's no mill close by, your best bet will be to purchase your stock at carving shows or to find outlets by joining local carving clubs.

Knives

MANY PEOPLE START OUT CARVING WITH a knife. Pocketknives, for example, can be relatively inexpensive, and their folding blades make them eminently portable; you can bring one with you for a small project you might want to whittle on vacation, for example.

When you're shopping for any knife, make sure it fits comfortably in your hand—you'll be holding it for long stretches. A small or thin-handled model can make your hands cramp after a while.

Pictured in the photo below are five of my favorites. Three are pocketknives I use every now and then in my general carving work. The white-handled knife at the bottom of the picture is a Case® Pocket

Whittler. This is a versatile, three-bladed jackknife for whittling, and it's readily available. A great all-around knife to start with, it feels good in your hand, and has a good selection of blades, but this one is not exactly how it came from the factory. Since they're easy to regrind, I often modify my carving knives, as I did with this one, slimming the blade for detail work.

The one on the far right is my old Remington knife. This is a universal kind of carving knife, with a long blade, a semi-rounded blade, and a flat blade. The handle is a little narrow for my liking.

The two-bladed Ross Oar knife, second from the right in the photo, has a comfortable handle and

quality steel. Its wide blade, however, makes it better for long, flat, straight cuts than for fine, curving work.

After you learn some of the basics of carving by using a knife, you'll probably graduate to other tools for much of your work. You may find that your experience is similar to mine—even though I have a whole collection of knives, I really only use one style for general carving. That's a detail knife, for such things as eyes, eyelids, nostrils, ears, fingers, undercutting, and shadows.

Two of my detail knives are shown on the left side of the photo. They have narrow, pointed blades for tight radius cuts. The blades are also very thin; they make almost surgical incisions without wedging

MADE FOR CHIPS The specialized chip-carving knife features an angled blade. Its wide, sturdy blade is designed specifically for straight cuts, and its stocky handle is easy to grasp.

in and fracturing the wood. I shaped the ergonomic handles myself, so that their curves fit right into my hand, with a place for my index finger and a flat spot on top for my thumb if I really want to put some force behind the cut.

Gouges

A GOUGE IS ESSENTIALLY A CHISEL WITH its blade rolled to a curved cutting edge, and it's one of the two types of tools I do most of my carving with. (The other is the V-tool—see p. 8).

I like #11 gouges (see "Gouge and V-tool numbering" on p. 9). Also known as veiners, they are the most deeply curved tools available. Their radical sweep makes them more versatile than their shallower cousins. When you're first getting started and can't invest in a wide array of tools, you want the most use out of the fewest, and gouges provide that. For example, with a large, heavily curved gouge, you can plough straight ahead and remove wood quickly, but you also can lay the tool on its side where the curve levels out and make a shallow cut—creating an effect similar to that of a shallow #3 gouge. **(PHOTO A)**

I suggest you get a large rough-out tool. The 11/15 is what I use to quickly remove a lot of

A

A SELECTION OF #11 GOUGES (left to right): 11/15, 11/10, 11/4, and 11/3.

wood at the beginning of a project. As you refine your carving technique and get into progressively more detail, you'll need smaller and smaller gouges. The 11/10 is a good medium-size gouge. Then, of the smaller members of the #11 family, you'll need 4-mm and 3-mm versions for fine detail work.

I use a big, 30-mm, #2 gouge for leveling broad areas and getting rid of ridges and hollows left by deeper tools. Its blade is nearly flat so its corners won't dig in. But the main way I use this tool is upside down, for smoothing large rounded shapes quickly without resorting to sandpaper. That way they retain a carved look.

I prefer full-size gouges, rather than the more limited-application palm tools. You can use full-size gouges one-handed, two-handed, or with a mallet. Swiss gouges are probably the finest carving tools available today. They come in the greatest variety of shapes and sizes, and the steel is fabulous. It holds an edge for the most delicate work, and has the strength and durability to take aggressive torquing when removing lots of wood quickly. These tools have held up for me for almost four decades. (See "Resources" on p. 184 for suppliers.)

V-tools

THE BLADE OF A V-TOOL, OR V-PARTING tool, looks just like its name—two bevel-edged chisel blades that meet in a V formation.

That cutting edge, available in a variety of angles, makes these tools indispensable for grooving, adding details and textures, and creating outlines and definition between shapes. V-tools are great for making curving, elongated lazy S-cuts. For this use, I modify the tool to take some of the heaviness out of the blade, so it will slide through the slot it's creating (see "Sharpening V-tools" on p. 34). The illustration on the facing page, "Relative curvatures, gouges," compares the configurations of several sizes.

The numbering of V-tools is not quite as standardized as that for gouges. The ones I give here are for the Swiss tools I use. Turning to the tools in the photo at right, the 12/10 V-tool is a comfortable midsize tool with a fairly wide V. The height of its shoulders allows you to make deep cuts in one swipe, but despite its size, you can still hold this tool with one hand. It's great for roughing out and outlining bold features, like arms, shoulders, legs, collars, hat brims, and so on.

The next smallest V-tool (immediately right

THREE ALL-PURPOSE V-TOOLS (left to right): 12/10, 15/6, and 16/3.

of the 12/10) is the #15 in a 6-mm width. The #15 comes in only two sizes, 6 mm and 3 mm (so the one shown is the largest size). You'll notice the angle is tighter than in the 12/10, but the sides are almost the same height. You can still cut fairly deeply with this, yet maintain a narrow V-cut for dramatic shadows that accentuate your forms and add depth. This tool also performs well for a little finer roughing out, and for defining and refining body features, as well as for carving hair, beard, and feather textures.

GOUGE AND V-TOOL NUMBERING

Carving tools are identified by two numbers, often stamped on the handle or the upper part of the blade.

The first relates to a standard numbering system which describes the curvature or sweep of the blade. The second number is the width across the open part of the blade, measured in either millimeters or fractions of an inch.

For example, in the collection shown at right, the "8/7" designation stamped on the gouge in the middle means that it's a #8 gouge and it's 7 mm wide. The designation of gouges runs from 1 through 11, with #1 being dead flat like a chisel and #11 having the deepest curve.

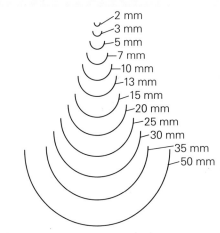

IT'S ALL IN THE NUMBERS
Carving tools come in many shapes, from flat to U-shaped. They rely on a numbering system to differentiate one shape and size from another.

Relative curvatures, gouges

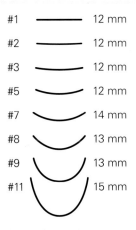

#1	12 mm
#2	12 mm
#3	12 mm
#5	12 mm
#7	14 mm
#8	13 mm
#9	13 mm
#11	15 mm

All gouges of the same number don't actually have sweeps of the same arc. Rather, the number refers to the diameter of the arc relative to the size of the tool. In the diagram below, you see that the sweeps of #9 gouges roughly resemble a half circle. But the curve of a 3-mm tool comes from a 3-mm ($1/8$-in.) circle, while a 50-mm gouge has the sweep of a 50-mm (about 2-in.) circle. Thus all the #9 gouges are relatively deep-sweep tools; if they all had the same arc as the 50 mm does, the 3-mm gouge would be almost flat. V-tools achieve different profiles depending on the relationship of their size, the width of the "V" at its widest part, and the angle formed at its radius.

V-tool numbering system

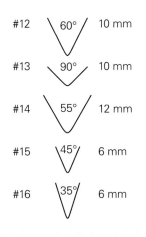

#12	60°	10 mm
#13	90°	10 mm
#14	55°	12 mm
#15	45°	6 mm
#16	35°	6 mm

Sweeps: #9 gouges

2 mm
3 mm
5 mm
7 mm
10 mm
13 mm
15 mm
20 mm
25 mm
30 mm
35 mm
50 mm

Then, for creating finer textures, you'll need a 16/3 V-tool. The angle of this tool is narrower yet. The #16 comes in the same two sizes as the #15 (so the one shown in the photo on p. 8 is the smallest available). But what is nice about this Swiss tool is that, since the angle is so narrow, even the tiny 3-mm width between the tips still leaves you with a fairly high-walled tool. Most other small, detail V-tools are only half the height of this one. This one is more versatile. You can cut shallow surface textures for beards, hair, fur, or feathering, and you also can cut deeper—for undercutting and creating shadows—without cracking and tearing the wood.

STORING YOUR TOOLS

Sharp cutting edges are fragile, so it's important to protect them. Don't store the tools in a damp environment or where they'll be jostled against each other.

A damp environment will promote rust and so will padding the blades with cork—it can seal in moisture. A wooden box doesn't hold moisture like a plastic box. I crisscross my tools in the drawers, as shown in the photo at right, so the tips don't bang against each other when I travel.

I also have a box for all my sharpening stones and leather strops, which keeps them in good shape and ensures they don't get lost. You may also notice that I paint a portion of my handles and I woodburn my name on them. I travel all over the country conducting seminars, and I'm not the only one who owns Swiss tools. So to make sure I go home with the ones that are mine, I mark them so that I can see them easily. If I lend a tool, my name reminds the friend it's mine.

If you don't have a carving-tool box, get an inexpensive cloth tool roll, like the one shown in the photo at left. Its individual pockets separate and protect the blades and keep them organized. Roll the whole thing up and secure it with the attached ties. You can even take your tools with you on vacation (just don't try to get them past airport security).

Power carving tools

POWER CARVING IS A FUN WAY TO
experiment with a different approach to carving.
Your work progresses quickly, and there are many
unique effects you can only get with this technique.
For example, I've recently developed a method of
carving realistic wildlife figures with power tools
(see "Power Carving and Woodburning" on p. 142).

Power carving is an option for those who want
to carve without mastering hand-tool sharpening
techniques. It also helps people with arthritis and
others who just don't have the stamina to hold carving tools firmly for any length of time.

Power carving tools and equipment are available
through carving supply shops, catalogs, vendors at
trade shows, and on the Internet. (See p. 184 for
suppliers.)

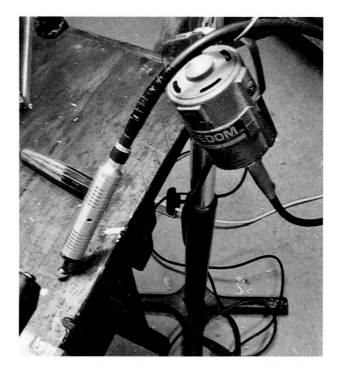

Flexible-shaft tools

The flexible-shaft tool shown in the photo, above
right, is the basis of power carving. It consists of a
powerful hanging motor that spins a rotating flexible shaft. A foot pedal controls the variable speed,
and a comfortable handpiece that clicks into the
shaft accepts a wide variety of cutters and carbide
burrs and bits. The collection shown in the photo
at right, is just a sample of what's available.

Equipped with a coarse carbide burr, this tool
can hog out an almost frightening amount of material very rapidly. It's a supremely useful tool, but
warrants great respect and caution.

Several manufacturers make these carvers,
including Mastercarver®, and the one I use,
Foredom®. I find it helpful to have more than one
handpiece, and I often load each with a different
bit when starting a project. That way, I can easily
change cutting bits as I work.

Micro-motor hand grinder

For finer detail work, I recommend a lighter micro-motor hand grinder. The motor is encased in the handpiece, so the tool is easier to control and works with very little vibration. The photo at right shows my Ultima handpiece, a model which combines a micro-motor tool with a woodburning tool. It has a variable speed that tops out at 45,000 rpm. (See "Resources" on p. 184.)

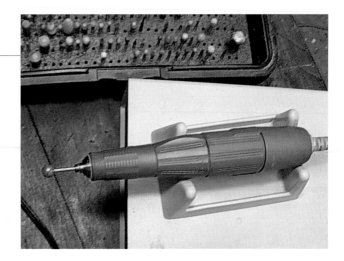

Woodburners

A woodburner consists of an electrically heated stylus enclosing a tip whose heat burns the wood to create designs and textures. Most of the good units have a variable temperature control. Some woodburners have a single handpiece and employ interchangeable tips. The Ultima system I use is different. Each handpiece and tip is a single apparatus. The handpieces with interchangeable tips tend to heat up and become a little uncomfortable as you hold them, whereas integral units like the one I use do not.

Various types of tips will yield various effects. I like a knife tip, as it's basically the same design as my detail-knife blades. I actually designed a variation, called the Sabol Skew, (bottom right, in the photo above) with an extended reach for getting into deeper areas.

Carver's vises

From a simple, fixed carver's screw to elaborate, 360°-rotating work positioners, these devices mount to your benchtop and stabilize your carving so that you can work with both hands. A good carver's vise or work positioner should be sturdy, secure, and

adjustable in all three axes (up and down, back and forth, and side to side). There are many high-quality brands. I use a Jerry-Rig® model, shown above, which was designed by a carver and combines unlimited positioning with rock-solid rigidity.

Collecting dust

If you're going to do much power carving, you'll want a dust collector. The one shown, right, is a dual-fan dust collector equipped with a furnace filter to capture the dust. When I'm doing a large piece, I'll add a Shop-Vac®, set up in tandem, to create even more draw.

Make sure your dust collection system is placed as close as possible to your power carving station so the system gathers all the dust from your work. Otherwise, the dust will cover you and spread to the rest of the room. Be sure to wear a dust mask, also.

Tool techniques

IN THIS SECTION I'LL DEMONSTRATE carving techniques specific to various tools. The instructions are written for the right-handed carver (to match the carver in the photos—me). If you're left-handed, just reverse the instructions.

Safety, of course, is paramount. Always be aware of where your fingers are, who's next to you, the direction of the cutting edge, and the amount of pressure you're putting behind the blade. Carving is intentional—it's using a specific tool to make a specific cut to produce a specific result.

If you get only one thing out of this book, I'd like it to be how you make a slicing cut with all tools. Perfecting that technique begins by practicing it with a knife. The slice is the basis of carving and provides its magic. The idea is to use a slicing motion that engages the entire length of a tool's cutting edge. Rather than pushing the tool straight through the wood like a plow, slicing shears the wood as if it were milk chocolate. If you can get this motion to be second nature, carving will become a pleasurable experience you can do for hours without fatigue.

Carving with a knife

There are two basic techniques in knife carving— the pivot cut and the paring cut. If you practice until you become comfortable with both of them, you'll be able to handle most any freehand whittling challenge that comes your way.

For a pivot cut, place the thumb of your left hand up against the back of the blade **(PHOTO A)**, so that both hands are in contact with the blade at all times.

Use the left thumb as a pivot for the blade, pushing and controlling as you cut with a slicing motion.

The paring cut is a motion similar to peeling an apple. Using your right hand, grasp the knife with

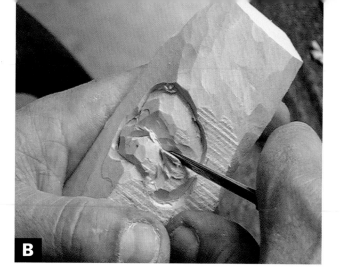

B

the blade facing you. Pivot your right thumb against the piece you are carving as you slice into the wood by closing your fist and drawing the blade in a slicing movement toward you. Keep your thumb out of the path of the blade **(PHOTO B)**.

Using a gouge

Using a gouge in carving work also relies on two techniques—the backhand grip and the forehand grip. No matter which one you employ, you'll want to keep your carving hand close to the blade.

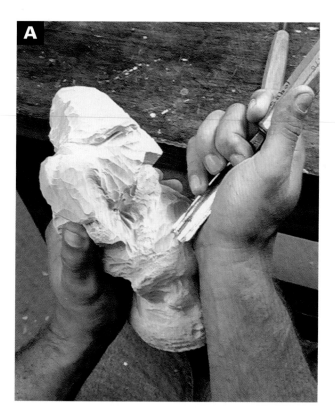

A

Because a full-length gouge has a long handle and a lot of reach, you won't have much control, power, or leverage if you hold the tool back on the handle.

USING A BACKHAND GRIP

1. For the backhand grip, choke up on the chisel, holding it diagonally through the palm of your right hand. Rest it between your forefinger and thumb, and curl your remaining fingers around it so that only about ¾ in. sticks out below your hand. Hold the carving in your left hand and rest the edge of your right hand on the wood. To begin the cut, roll your right wrist up and bring the blade into contact with the wood **(PHOTO A)**.

2. Roll your right wrist down **(PHOTO B)** to make the cut. You can see exactly where the chisel is going, and it can't go any further because your right hand butts against the wood to stop it. Assuming your blade is sharp, you're exerting very little force, just finesse. Just rock your wrist, chipping away small chips like a beaver chewing, and the wood just melts away efficiently and safely.

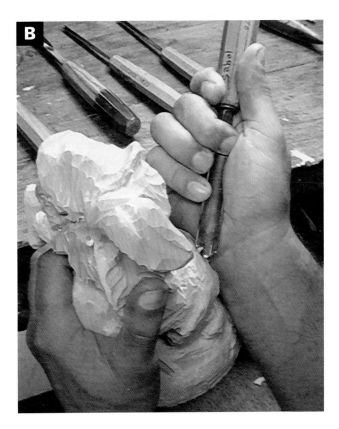

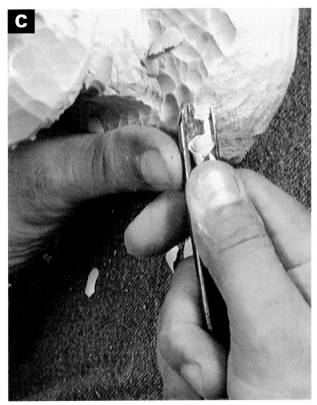

USING A FOREHAND GRIP

With the forehand grip, the carving action will move away from you.

3. Again, you'll really want to choke up on the blade **(PHOTO C)**. Curl your right index finger under the back of the shaft, and hold your right thumb on top—about 1 to 1½ inches away from the cutting edge. Rest your left thumb on the side of the blade. You'll use it as a pivot.

4. As you begin the cut, push the blade into the wood and being to roll the gouge in a slicing motion. Continue rolling the tool along the curvature of the cutting edge, applying a slight forward pressure to keep the tool in the wood. Twist your forearm, not just the wrist; as soon as your index finger touches the carving, you should be out of the cut **(PHOTO D)**.

Carving with a V-tool

Although the configuration of a V-tool is different than a gouge, gripping the V-tool with your hand close to the cutting edge is equally important. The proximity of your hand to the edge determines how much control you'll have when making the cut. You can't roll the V-tool in one smooth slicing motion as you can the rounded cutting edge of a gouge, of course, but the essential motion is the same.

1. Rest your right wrist on the carving (**PHOTO A**). Applying forward pressure to the blade, slice the wood with an arc and a slight twist. Move your wrist back and forth to make S-cuts.

2. To provide a measure of safety and control, keep your right hand against the carving. The cut will stop when your fingers contact the wood (**PHOTO B**).

3. You can achieve a great deal of control by turning the piece into the cutting edge at the same time (**PHOTO C**). Pivot the carving against your right hand with forward pressure on the tool.

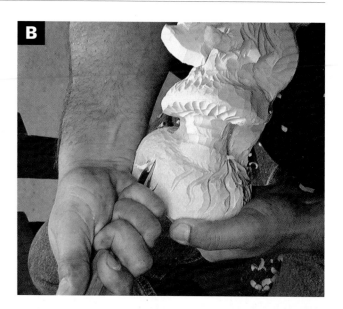

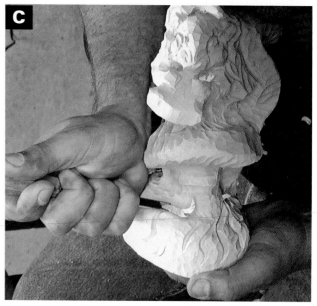

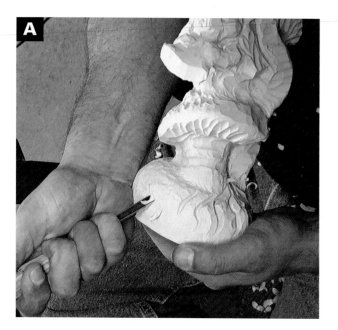

WORK SMART

Practice these techniques and think about what you're doing with each stroke so that every cut you make is intentional. Your tools will create shapes that reside in your mind, your heart, and your soul. Your carvings will reflect you. Have fun.

Changing the direction of a cut is clearly demonstrated (and easier to accomplish) with a smaller instrument like the 16/3 V-tool. Grasp the shaft of the blade between your right thumb and index finger. Then wrap the other fingers of your right hand around the blade and handle so you can roll the tool by opening and closing your hand, using your thumb as a pivot point.

Start off with your hand open, and as you close it and pivot on the thumb, the cutting edge automatically swings to the right **(PHOTO D)**. To make the tool go off to the left, start the cut and roll out your fingers the other way **(PHOTO E)**. You're out of the cut as soon as you can't spin your wrist anymore and the tool won't go any further.

You can accentuate the S-curves by turning the carving and the tool together while you swing your hand either open or closed. This is how to get those lively, tight arcs and curves in beard and fur texture **(PHOTO F)**.

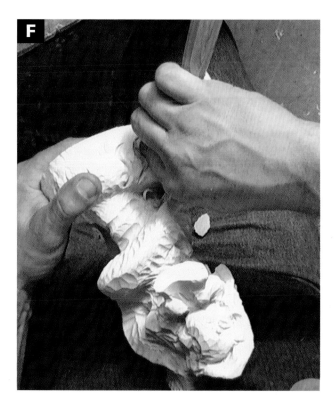

Suggested woods

OF THE VAST ARRAY OF LUMBER species commonly available, only a few are prime carving woods. You can obtain good-quality carving wood from a variety of sources. Some local specialty lumberyards and even sawmills will sell you wood. There are many mail-order suppliers. Carving shows and local carving clubs all over this country have information on where to get wood. (You can find carving clubs on the Internet, through local carving magazines, at senior or civic centers, or by speaking to other carvers.)

It's best to buy from local sources so you can pick out exactly what you want. To make your carving easier and more successful, start off with the best wood you can find. Wood, like anything else, has a personality. Some wood will be very cooperative, and some will fight you all the way.

When I am picking out carving wood, one rule of thumb I use is weight. When I have two pieces of about equal size, whichever one weighs less is generally the one I want to carve, as it'll be less dense.

PRIME CARVING WOODS Shown here are three of the most popular carving woods (left to right): white pine, basswood, and tupelo.

When I go to a sawmill to buy a log, I look for a specific grain pattern and coloration in the wood, which I'll describe in the sections that follow. When you're shopping at a lumberyard or sawmill, bring along a gouge or a small handplane. Take a little swipe of the end grain to get an idea of what it looks like. If you're purchasing a whole log, you can cut it apart on the bandsaw when you get home to find the best sections to work with.

Basswood

The most popular, the most commonly known, and the most readily available carving wood throughout the country today is basswood. It has a pleasing and unobtrusive white color, a very uniform grain, and it carves like butter—both with and across the grain. It holds detail very well and has a lot of strength, so you can carve fairly thin forms that won't be too fragile. Some of the best basswood comes from Minnesota, but you can find it at almost any carving supply shop anywhere in the United States.

Try to find a basswood piece that has a very light or "white" color. Basswood with a grayish or dark color tends to be gritty and will prove much more difficult to work. The best wood is cut during the wintertime. Summer-cut wood is darker, denser, and more difficult to carve.

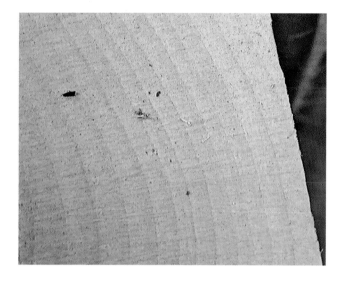

Look at the end grain of a piece of basswood. As shown in the photo at left, when the grain lines are spaced fairly well apart, there are fewer fibers between the growth rings. A tight-grained piece of basswood will be denser and harder to carve.

Basswood is probably the most versatile carving wood. Not only does it carve beautifully with hand tools, it also accepts power carving and woodburning quite well, if you want to use those techniques to add texture. Its light color and non-prominent grain pattern also work wonderfully with the thinned-oil painting method I describe in this book.

White pine

My wood of choice for the past 30 years has been northern white pine. I carve it when it's freshly cut and not yet dried—a condition known as wet or green wood. Northern white pine is readily available in the Northeast, and you can probably order it in several other parts of the country as well. If you can get some, you owe it to yourself to try carving this wonderful material.

The grain of white pine is much more visible than basswood grain (shown below, left). Once again, look

for widely spaced growth rings and lighter colors, as shown below, right. Overall, the redder, darker wood is going to be harder and less pleasant to carve.

White pine is a beautiful wood to carve wet. When it's dry, it tends to want to run and splinter and split, but when it's wet, a knife will just sing right through it. The moisture in the wood reduces the drag on your tool, giving you a smoother and cleaner cut.

The wet wood is also more pliable. It's not as brittle and prone to breakage as kiln-dried wood, and it can take a tremendous amount of detail. That has allowed me to create pieces I probably couldn't have produced from basswood or other carving species.

I have often carved complex figures out of a single piece of wood—creations with difficult undercuts, and birds in flight with intricately splayed feathers. The pliability of the wood allowed my knife to slide through with little force, lifting, separating, and shearing delicate details that would have snapped and broken off with dry wood.

The piece shown in the photo above, which I call "Daddy's Hat," is a carving I did of my son when he was about a year and a half old. It's probably the most photographed piece I've ever done. I carved it from soaking-wet white pine—when I put my gouge into the wood, water was actually squishing out of it. I carved this piece in 1991, and there's no checking or cracking, even after drying and being battered around all these years.

One other aspect of carving wet wood is that you can get it so thin you can shine a light through it and gauge its thickness as you carve. I've been able to get bird feathers, flowers, flower petals, and leaves paper-thin. They glow in the translucent light.

You can take a piece of air-dried or kiln-dried white pine and soak it. But on a scale of 1 to 10, with 10 being how pine carves when green, I'd say that air dried and soaked, it never reaches more than a 6 or 7. It never achieves the same desirability of a freshly cut piece, because after the fibers shrink, they don't expand back to their full size even when you moisten them. For the ultimate carving experience, the best time to carve wet white pine is as soon as possible after the tree hits the ground.

For that reason, I store my pine outside—no shed or anything, just in the open, covered with snow. When it's frozen, it can't lose moisture. I cut it on the bandsaw and then put it in the microwave to defrost it. (I don't do this when my wife is home.) In the summertime I just cover it with a plastic tarp. And if it's a real dry summer, I'll spray it down once or twice a week with the hose.

Tupelo

Tupelo comes out of Louisiana and the Southern swamps. It's a surprisingly lightweight wood (shown on the facing page, left), but it has a tremendous amount of strength and lends itself very well to power carving. It's not a good wood to carve with hand tools. No matter how sharp your knife or gouge is, the wood always tends to tear or crumble.

Tupelo is a favorite of bird carvers, as they primarily use power. For power carving, this wood is absolutely phenomenal. It holds minute detail and its strength is unsurpassed for creating thin, delicate, realistic flowers and animals.

In selecting pieces of wood for the best carving qualities, the grain rings can fool you. It's best to rely on the weight rule, and select the lightest piece. A heavier, denser piece of tupelo tends to want to burn rather than grind away, creating burn marks and ruining your finer stones and carving bits.

The piece shown at right is one of my power-carved creations from a single tupelo block, with the thorns carved from bamboo and added later. As you can see, the detail tupelo can hold is incredible. It finishes up beautifully and accepts my oil painting techniques well.

Cherry and black walnut

Cherry (shown at right) and black walnut (shown bottom, right) are beautiful woods, and, because of their color and sheen, they are very popular to carve for projects with a natural finish.

They are much harder, denser woods, and thus are not the best species to start with for a beginner. Since it takes more force to work harder wood, your tools need to be extremely sharp to avoid accidents and to keep the tools cutting smoothly and safely.

There is no point going to the extra effort of carving cherry or walnut for a painted piece, but they'll create a spectacular natural-finish carving. The carved surface has a very attractive burnish or luster to it. And there's nothing like the aroma these woods give off as you work them.

Sharpening Your Tools

PROPER TOOL SHARP-ening is one of the most important aspects of carving.

Dull tools can hinder even the most enthusiastic carver, turning a pleasant pastime into a frustrating experience.

Razor-sharp tools are necessary for carving. You'll get a keen cutting edge by using a progression of stones to wear away microscopic bits of metal from the blade, leaving behind tiny serrations in its edge. The job of each successive stone is to replace the coarser serrations with increasingly finer ones. Part of the finesse involved in honing a tool is getting these serrations regularly distributed across the cutting edge.

In this chapter, I'll show you how to achieve the finest possible edges so you'll get the optimum performance from all of your carving tools. It takes a little practice. Don't get frustrated if it doesn't work quite the way you want the first time. It took me a while to acquire the skills too, but it's really not hard.

THERE ARE MANY KINDS OF SHARPENING stones available: Japanese water stones, ceramic stones, diamond stones, and diamond boards. I find the best and most efficient type is the time-honored natural Arkansas stones used with oil. I've arranged a few of them and some strops in the photo on the facing page.

The small grayish brown stone in the middle is called a soft Arkansas. The white one above it is a hard white Arkansas, and the large dark one at bottom left is a hard black Arkansas—the finest stone money can buy. The softest and coarsest natural stone of all is the Washita, shown in the photo at right.

To hone your tools, you need to progress to gradually finer abrasive surfaces—from a coarse (soft) stone to a medium stone to a fine (hard) stone, and then to a leather strop. A stone has sharp microscopic particles on its surface that stick up like tines on a rake. They tear away little shards of metal from the tool's cutting edge. A coarse stone tears away larger particles, leaving relatively deep grooves. Smoother stones make smaller, but more numerous scratches. As you move to finer and finer stones, you start to refine and level out those deep peaks and valleys you created with the coarser stones.

A leather strop is a piece of leather that is usually adhered to a flat hardwood stick or board. In the photo on the facing page there is a flat strop with white pigskin leather (second from the top in the photo, and years of use have turned it to a dull gray), and a universal strop made for gouges and V-tools, with hollows, humps, and fins for inside and outside surfaces (top of the photo). The universal strop is used with buffing compound to put the final razor edge and mirror polish on your tools.

You'll need a bottle of honing oil. The oil acts as a lubricant and keeps all the little metal filings floating. Without the oil, the steel particles shorn off the blade would clog the pores of the stone. It would become glazed and incapable of cutting. As the oil fills with metal particles, wipe it off with a rag occasionally to keep the surface of your stone clean, sharp, and cutting as efficiently and effectively as possible.

SOFT STONE **The Washita stone is the softest of the oilstone family. Whatever kind of stone you use, you'll start with your softest stone when honing many of your tools.**

Resharpening

JUST AS IMPORTANT AS SHARPENING IS recognizing when you need to resharpen. You can't become complacent once you do have a good sharp tool. It becomes dull with use and needs to be periodically touched up as you work.

I'm often asked, "How often do you sharpen your tools?" The answer is, "Whenever they need it," because there isn't any set amount of time that an edge lasts. For one tool on one project, an edge could dull after five or ten minutes, but on another project, the edge might last all day. You'll find, however, that the tool itself will tell you when it needs sharpening.

When it's sharp, a tool slides through the wood with very little effort, slicing the fibers and leaving a beautiful, smooth surface. After a while, the surface looks a little cloudy, and you might start seeing some slight streaks or tearout in the wood. The wood fights you a bit, and it becomes harder to push the tool through. You can hear the gentle swish of a clean slice change to the scratching, gritty sound of tearing fibers.

When you suspect your edge is ready for rejuvenation, don't hesitate. Look closely at the surface of the cut and the edge of the tool (see "Track Marks" on p. 36). It's faster and easier to touch up a tool that's just beginning to dull than to resharpen a tool from scratch. Sometimes all you need to do is run the edge over your hardest stone.

HONING ESSENTIALS

When sharpening a tool, you need to make sure you've honed the bevel evenly and completely before you progress to the next finest stone. From time to time, wipe the blade clean and sight along it into a light to gauge how your bevel is coming along. You're looking for three things:

1. You want a flat, even bevel. The reflection of light will tell you if you've been changing the angle while honing **(PHOTO A)**. Any deviation from flat will show as a facet, like the face of a diamond. Check both sides of a knife blade. They should be even and similar, but they don't necessarily have to be equally wide. I tend to lean a little on one side, so all my knives have one bevel slightly wider, but it doesn't matter, as long as both are flat. Each finer stone smooths the larger scratches left by the previous stone, and you can see the difference. Don't change stones till the entire bevel is uniform.

2. On a gouge, if the angle established with one stone is slightly different than the last one, you may see a small band of coarser sheen **(PHOTO B)**. That's OK, as long as the two angles are close to the same and the bevel is ground evenly all along its length.

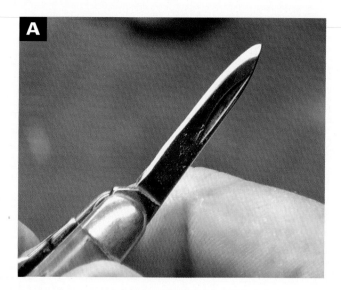

Resurfacing worn stones

NATURAL STONES EVENTUALLY ERODE AS you run steel over them. At some point, sometimes over a period of several years, they will get worn down in the middle, as you see in the photo of an older stone at right. It becomes more difficult to get a flat bevel on your tools with a cupped stone. The softer the stone, the more prone it is to this bellying. For example, while a soft Arkansas wears more quickly, a hard black Arkansas is so dense that I've had mine for about 30 years and can't notice any hollowing at all. You can reflatten stones by rubbing them across a flat steel plate with abrasive paste.

3. You want a consistent burr. Each honing brings the two surfaces on either side of the cutting edge closer to each other. When they finally meet, one starts to curl over the other, creating a thin, fragile burr, also referred to as a wire edge. On a knife, it builds up on the side opposite the one you've just honed. On a gouge or V-tool it's on the inside. You can feel it: pull the blade backward across your finger (opposite the cutting direction), and you'll feel the burr drag on your skin.

Since the intersecting surfaces are raked with fine scratches, the burr feels serrated. Before you move on to the next stone, keep honing until the burr runs the length of the blade. Each stone will remove the burr from the previous stone and create a new, finer burr. Then the strop will finally remove the burr, leaving a strong, sharp edge.

B

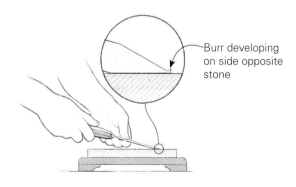

Burr developing on side opposite stone

Knives

A POCKETKNIFE IS A GOOD TOOL TO START with to learn sharpening skills. In honing against a stone, you're creating a bevel that supports the cutting edge of the tool. You want a fairly low angle for the least cutting resistance, but you don't want the bevel too wide or it will be brittle and snap off.

It's important to keep a consistent blade-to-stone angle while honing so that the bevel grinds flat and even. For that reason, I don't hone in a circular motion, because I can't keep a consistent angle. If you change the angle, you tend to round the bevel, which creates more drag as you carve. That causes you to hold the knife on a higher angle, which drives it down into the wood so you are constantly fighting the knife as you cut.

1. The first step in honing begins with a soft, coarse stone. This cuts quickly, removes imperfections, and resurfaces the cutting edge. I start with a Washita. Put a little oil on the surface of the stone, **(PHOTO A)**, and spread it with your finger.

2. You want a very slight tilt to the blade. Lay a dime on the stone. To gauge the proper angle, hold the knife so the bottom of its back edge is about even with the top of the coin **(PHOTO B)**.

3. Take a firm grip on the knife with your right thumb on the side of the blade, keeping your right hand close to the cutting edge for maximum control. Hold the knife at this angle as steadily as possible and with the cutting edge facing you, draw the knife toward you **(PHOTO C)**. Think of the action as trying to shave a thin slice off the stone. As you finish the stroke, and without stopping,

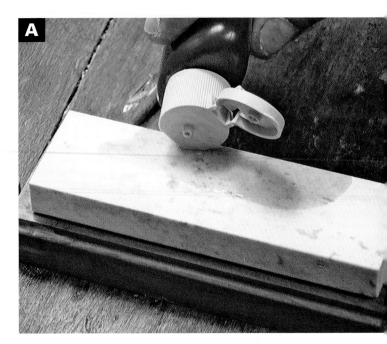

raise the blade so the tip makes contact with the stone **(PHOTO )**. That way, you'll sharpen the entire length of the blade, including the tip, at the same angle.

Repeat this process on the first edge several times, holding the knife at a consistent angle and pulling it toward you. Try not to let your wrist rock. Keep it locked in one position. Every time you put the blade back on the stone, feel for the flatness of the bevel and settle it right back to that same angle, so the bevel doesn't start to round off.

4. Flip the blade to hone the other side. This time, set the tip of the knife on the end of the stone closest to you **(PHOTO 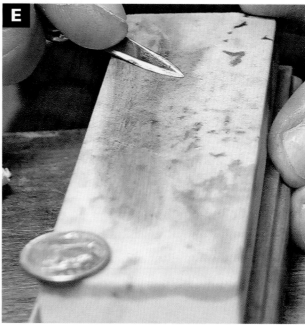)** and push the knife across the stone away from you, lowering the blade as you complete this pass to bring the length of the cutting edge in contact with the stone **(PHOTO 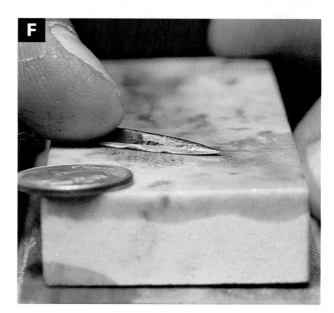)**. Hone this edge with several passes. Then hone each edge in alternate passes, using the same number of strokes on each side. Pretty soon, you'll start to get into a rhythm.

Wipe the blade with a rag to check your progress. Look at the bevel's reflection—you want a nice flat surface developing evenly on both sides. Feel for the burr. Once the burr has come up on the entire cutting edge and the bevels are flat and even, it's time to refine the edge with the next stone.

To get a true reading of how sharp your blade is, make a cut in the edge of a board. You can tell a blade is dull and needs to be sharpened when it crushes and tears the wood fibers. You want a smooth, burnished cut.

Refining the edge

To refine the edge, you'll move to the soft Arkansas stone, then to the hard white Arkansas, and then to a leather strop.

1. Smear a few drops of oil on the soft Arkansas stone. Follow the same honing technique you used on the previous stone, alternately pulling one edge toward you and raising the tip and pushing the other edge away from you, starting at the tip **(PHOTO A)**. Hone each side of the blade several times. There's no magic formula, but it'll probably take about 25 to 30 strokes on each side, depending on your technique and the condition of the blade.

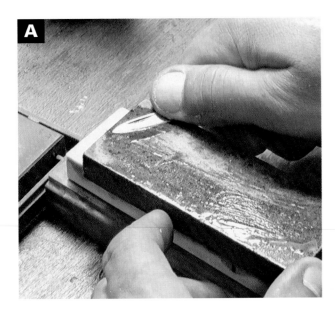

WORK SMART

To test the sharpness of a blade, don't run your finger down the edge. Lay the blade on your thumbnail. If the blade is still dull it will slide, but if it's sharp, it's going to catch and not slide off.

2. Switch to the hard white Arkansas stone **(PHOTO B)** and, using the same strokes, refine the edge even more. Now you're starting to put a fine edge on the blade. When you've taken it as far as you can on this stone, move to the hard black Arkansas with a thin film of oil. This is the final stone you'll use. It may feel like it's doing absolutely nothing, like honing on plate glass, but you're smoothing those scratches and putting a very keen edge on the knife.

You can't just go from the hard black Arkansas to carving. The burr would break off and take a little bit of the blade with it, so instead we're going to go to the next honing step: a leather strop with buffing compound.

3. Wipe the oil from your hands and the knife. Rub buffing compound on the leather **(PHOTO C)**. Lay the bevel of the knife flat on the leather and draw the knife backward across the strop.

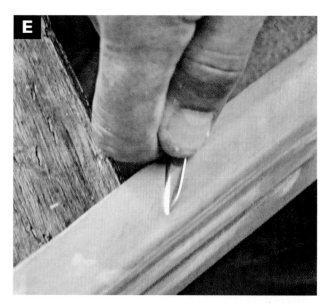

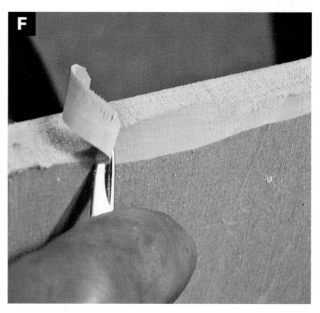

As you can see, honing with oil-stones gets messy. When you're done sharpening, wash your hands and wipe your tools down well with a clean rag so that you don't transfer the oil and grit to your carvings.

4. After a few strokes on both sides of the blade, you'll notice a shine developing on the leather (**PHOTO D**). What you see are microscopic particles of steel that were in the burr and have been removed by the compound.

5. Once you can't feel the burr catching when you stroke the blade, you're finished. But if you really want to put the ultimate edge on the blade, use a raw leather strop without compound (**PHOTO E**).

6. Now it's time to take the blade for a test drive across the edge grain to see how well the knife cuts. What you're looking for is a smooth, shiny burnish on the surface of the cut (**PHOTO F**).

Sharpening gouges

BECAUSE GOUGES HAVE A SINGLE BEVEL wrapped around their tip, they require a unique honing technique. I recommend honing gouges in the direction of the cutting edge instead of drawing and rolling the bevel sideways across the stone. I think it's harder to keep a consistently flat bevel if you hone the blade sideways, and the scratches are going to go across the bevel, creating more friction and drag.

Before you begin sharpening, make a test cut across the grain to see whether you have to start with a very coarse stone or just need to touch up the edge a little. You can see that the gouge shown below left is pulling badly in the center, leaving chewed-up areas and a cloudy surface. This is a dull tool needing serious work.

1. Spread oil on your coarsest stone. Using your right hand, hold the gouge with a firm grip and choke up on the blade. Set the bevel flat against the stone, and apply pressure with your left thumb downward on the gouge to the stone. As you push the gouge forward, move both hands with it. Maintain the same pressure as you push the tool down the length of the stone, rolling the gouge at the same time. By the end of the stroke, you should have engaged the full arc of the bevel **(PHOTOS A THROUGH C)**. Repeat this stroke until the bevel is ready for the next finest stone.

TESTING THE EDGE Making a test cut across the grain can tell you a lot about the condition of the cutting edge. Here, the dull edge of this gouge tears at the wood, indicating a need for some serious honing.

TIGHT TURNS This 11/10 gouge is an older tool. You can see it's not squared at the ends, and it's a little wobbly in places. As long as it cuts well, I don't particularly care if it's perfectly straight across. Rounding the corners of a gouge creates a narrow radius that makes tightly curved cuts easier.

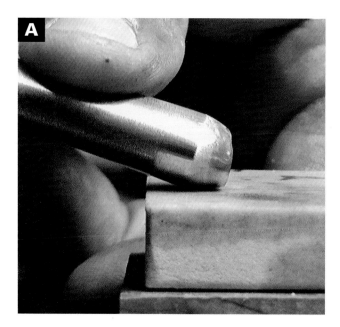

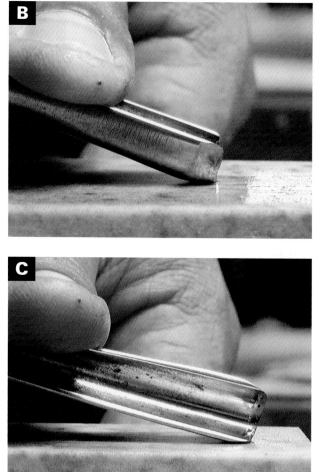

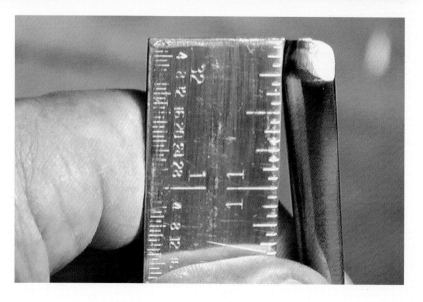

2. Every once in a while, clean the stone and put another drop or two of oil on it. Once you see a uniform dullness and an even burr on the bevel, move to the soft Arkansas, then to the hard white Arkansas, and on to the hard black Arkansas, using the techniques previously described for sharpening knives.

HOW LONG SHOULD THE BEVEL BE?

The length of the bevel on a gouge will be related to the size of the tool and will affect the ease with which it travels through the workpiece.

The bevel I generally put on my gouges ranges from about ¼ in. to ⁵⁄₁₆ in., but I might go all the way up to ⅜ in. on a really big tool. The longer the wedge and the lower the angle, the easier the tool slides through the wood. The more blunt the angle, the more force it requires.

Stropping a gouge

1. Shave off some of your buffing compound and spread it around in the grooves of the strop (**PHOTO A**). Rub the compound block on the tops of the humps, too.

2. Find the channel where the tool fits, and drag it backward, away from the cutting edge. In **PHOTO B**, the channel on the left was a bit too tight for the gouge.

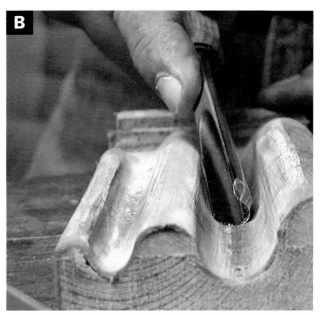

STOPPING ON A DIME

Honing carving tools is not a dainty operation. It takes both hands, and you want to put some force, weight, and twist into the tool so it is efficiently shaped by the stone. Therefore, the stone needs to be immobilized. You can use bench dogs or clamp a low wood block to your bench to stop the stone from moving. I tack a dime in the slit of my bench, so that the stone has something to rest up against. I also stand up when I sharpen my tools, so that I can put my weight into the task. If you like to sit down, maybe you could get a shorter table.

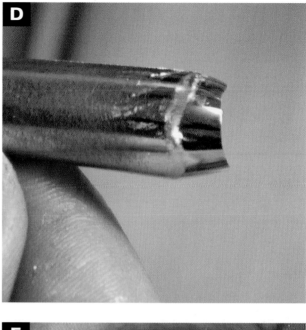

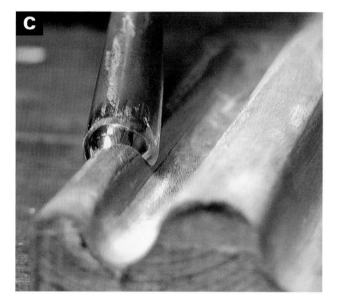

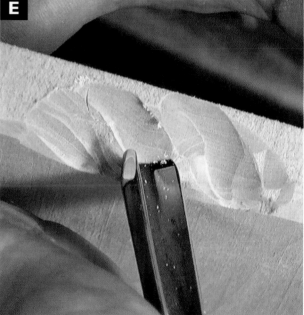

3. Then fit the hollow of the gouge on a ridge and
stroke the tool backward to remove the burr on the
inside of the tool **(PHOTO C)**. Put a fair amount of
pressure into the stropping to get the sweet edge
you're after. Notice that the leather on the strop
continues on both sides. I use buffing compound on
the right side and keep the left side clear. I finish by
stropping the bevel along the clear leather to put on
the final touch.

4. When you're finished, look at the reflection in
the edge. You should see that the scratches are all
gone and a beautiful polish remains **(PHOTO D)**.

5. Now we'll take it for a test ride. Remember all
the crushed wood fibers and dull finish on the cut
when we started? Take a cut across the grain and it
should display a nice burnish **(PHOTO E)**.

Sharpening V-tools

V-TOOLS ARE VERY USEFUL CARVING
instruments, but unfortunately, they don't come
carver friendly. The sides of the tool have a lot of
steel, which is necessary to properly support the
cutting edge. But that cutting edge is on the inside
of the V, and as you're cutting through the wood,
you're trying to stuff all the extra thickness of the
blade into the small incision that is being made by
the inside dimension of the tool **(PHOTO A)**.

A new V-tool out of the package has a pretty
steep bevel, and since all that steel can't fit into the
little slot the tool makes, when you try to make a
cut, the tool gets pinched out of the wood. To rem-
edy this, I grind the bevel down on a belt or disk
sander, increasing the bevel's taper and reducing the
bulk of the blade around the cutting edge. That way,
when I carve, I can bury the tool to its wings and
make a nice deep V-cut **(PHOTO B)**.

The procedure for sharpening a V-tool is
somewhat different than that for a gouge. A V-tool
is basically two knives tied together with a gouge
in between. You have a flat wing and a radius that
connects it to the other wing.

1. Use the same basic techniques you would
use to sharpen a gouge, pushing the cutting edge

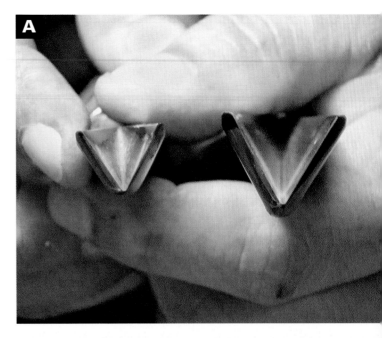

A

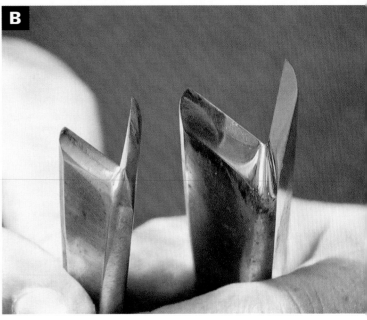

B

WORK SMART

On any tool, the burr curls backward on
the side opposite that being ground, so
drag your fingertip on the inside of the
bevel from the direction of the handle
to the tip. You should be able to feel the
burr coming up on the inside of the tool.
(Don't check from the cutting edge to
the handle—for obvious reasons.)

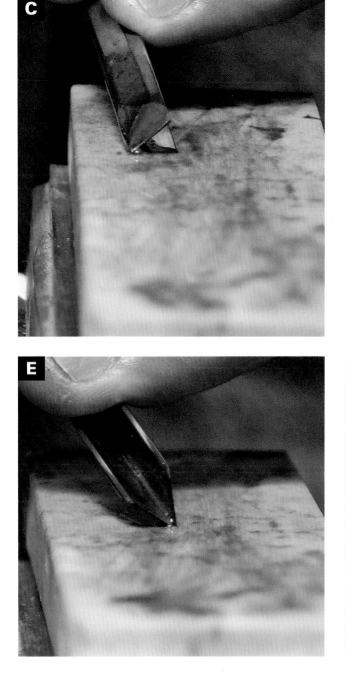

away from you down the stone. Start with the bevel flat on the stone, then about halfway down the stone, roll the blade, keep the tool moving, and continue on with the other flat side **(PHOTOS C THROUGH E)**.

If you concentrate on honing just the flat planes, the bottom of the "V" (the radius) will become fragile and prone to breaking, so you have to roll the chisel to sharpen the radius, too. As an alternative,

you can use shorter flat strokes and then roll the radius separately. This is a tricky tool to sharpen, but, as with the gouge, you're just sharpening the outside bevel surface.

2. Make a test cut, again going across the grain. If you've sharpened the tool properly, it will produce a crisp, sharp "V" without any tearing or pulling of the wood fibers **(PHOTO F)**.

TRACK MARKS

Take periodic test cuts in a scrap piece, then hold the tool in the light. Compare the surface of the cut (the track marks) with the condition of the cutting edge on the tool. You'll see exactly where the blade needs work. Here are some discrepancies to watch for the first few times you try sharpening:

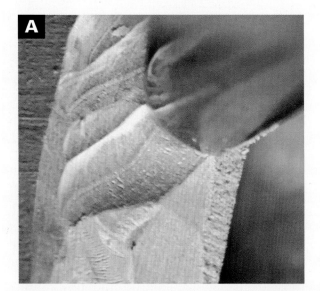

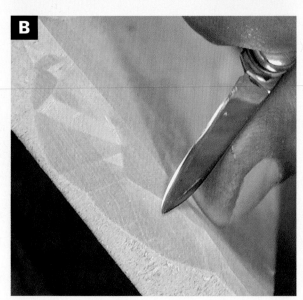

The left side of the gouge in **PHOTO A** looks pretty good, but the right side needs a little more honing.

A dull spot shows on the cut edge in **PHOTO B**. The blade's not too bad, but it doesn't quite have that shiny burnish. It has a sort of milky or cloudy surface. You might want to go back to the hard black Arkansas stone or you might just need to strop the blade a little more.

If you see serrated lines or a deeply embedded line or scratch, as in **PHOTO C**, there is still a piece of the burr hanging on the cutting edge and it's dragging across the surface of the cut.

If you see a raised white line on the face of the cut, that means there is a nick in the blade that's allowing wood to pass through without being cut. To get out such nicks, you'll probably have to go back to your coarse stone and start over.

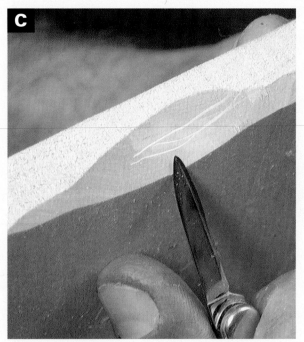

4. Start removing some of the wood around the top of the Santa's hood. As you progress around the carving, try to think about how all the parts are going to relate to one another, so that the carving evolves in a unified way. Widen the first triangular cut you made to form the foundation for the nose—the flare of the nostrils **(PHOTO D)**.

Whittling is a relaxing activity, and you should be in a comfortable position when doing it. Don't tense up and hunch over the work. You can sit back, but of course make sure your chair is stable and won't fall over.

CARVING AND GRAIN DIRECTION

When carving wood with a knife—or any other cutting tool—pay attention to the grain direction of the wood.

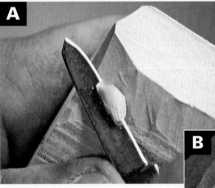

In a typical block of wood, the grain is oriented along the length of the material, and its texture runs primarily in one direction or the other.

When you carve with the grain **(PHOTO A)**, you are smoothing the fibers, and they will be severed cleanly. However, if you cut against the grain **(PHOTO B)**, you are ruffling the fibers, and

the wood will tend to tear, split, or chip out along the grain, into the finish surface of your carving.

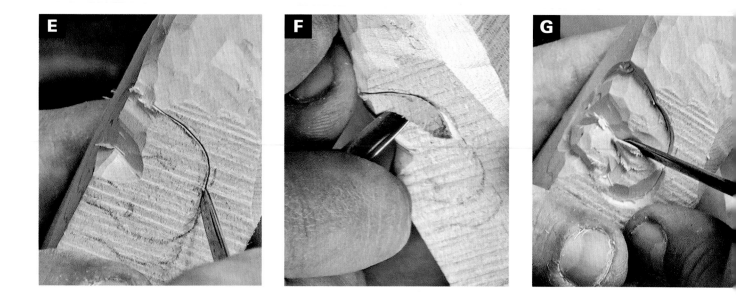

5. Make a deep, curving incision to outline the cheeks and the edge of the hood. Use your carefully controlled paring cut, keeping in mind the safety of your thumbs **(PHOTO E)**. This will be a stop cut, a defining cut to a desired depth, that will stop the next cut from going any deeper. When you make a cut from the opposite side, the chip will come out cleanly.

6. Slice along the other line of the cheek and remove the chip **(PHOTO F)**.

7. Make a little undercut on both sides to create eye sockets (once again, down from the top and then another cut up from below to meet it) **(PHOTO G)**. The beauty of using a small blade is that it allows you to make short curving cuts like this that can't be done with a big rough-out knife. Now you can continue forming the top of the hood.

Adding detail

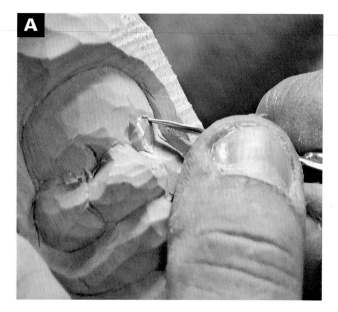

IT'S REALLY IMPORTANT TO HAVE A SHARP tip on your knife blade. Most of the cuts you'll make will start with the tip of the blade. If the tip is a little dull, you'll experience a lot of frustrating cracking and pulling.

In carving the facets and features on this project, make all of your cuts crisp and clean, removing any little fuzzies. Leave smooth finish cuts everywhere.

Use a few gently curving stop cuts to create the eyes.

1. Take the tip of the blade and make a fairly deep semicircular cut above the eye **(PHOTO A)**. Then make a very tight slit below the first cut, to create a V-cut. This will create an eyelid. Come underneath the eye and make the same type of cut you made above, then make another stop cut in the corner where the tear duct would be. Continue to round off and define the eyeball with the blade tip.

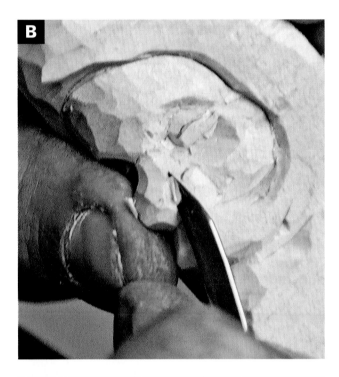

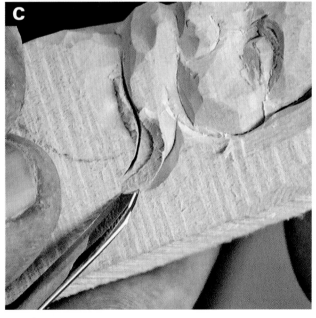

2. Now you can start shaping the nose, a triangular shape, narrower at the tip and flaring out at about a 45° angle from the center **(PHOTO B)**. That design will give Santa a well-shaped nose with plenty of room for nostrils. To form the side lobes of the nose, make a little hollow cut with the tip of the blade about halfway from the top of the nose to the cheek. Use the tip of the blade to create a little curving cut. Then remove the chip, and you'll have the makings of the wing of the nose. Continue to refine the shape of the nose and the cheek.

3. Follow the contours of the mustache with sweeping, curved stop cuts. Then make them into V-cuts to outline the mustache **(PHOTO C)**. Make a few cuts along the same lines to create some depth, so the mustache is really prominent and overhangs a bit. Remember, shadows really help punctuate shapes. Define the center of the mustache, and you can even bring a little V-cut right up to the tip of the nose to show the separation from the left and right mustache. Then use the tip of the blade to come around and take off any of the hard edges and soften it all up. You can further refine the eyes, any way you like.

LIGHT AND SHADOW

Light and shadow are very important to a carving. Shadows add depth and form and accentuate the shapes we create. While a shallow cut may hardly show up, deep cuts create the shadows that strengthen the forms and give the piece character and dimension. To make a carving interesting, use varying levels of depth, but be sure to incorporate lots of deep cuts.

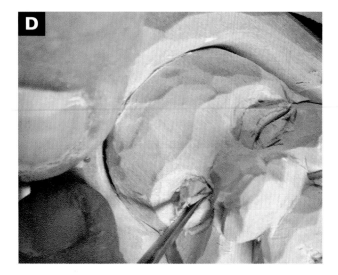

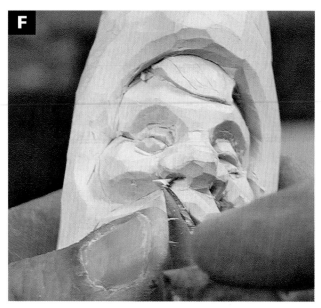

4. On this figure, I have carved the eyes closed **(PHOTO D)**, so I am going in with gently curving V-cuts to make the smiling separation between his eyelids. Little details give the face some character—maybe slight bags under his eyes, a few deep cuts to create crow's feet in the corners of the eyes, and laugh lines around his cheeks. Work on the eyebrows as well.

5. Now you can outline the beard with curving cuts. Round the beard off and undercut it a bit to give it a three-dimensional look. Go in and carve the rest of your figure as you've sketched it out. Give the fellow his hood and shape it to a bit of a peak. Let the fabric drape in a natural way.

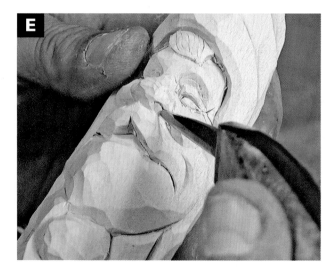

6. With the tip of the blade, make a semicircular cut to create the opening of the nostril **(PHOTO E)**.

7. Then come back and remove the little chip **(PHOTO F)**, so that a nice deep shadow accentuates the shapes on the face.

8. Cut a little opening for the mouth **(PHOTO G)**.

Finishing touches

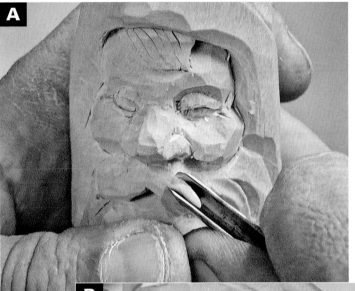

SO FAR, WE'VE DONE THIS WHOLE carving with just a jackknife blade. You can certainly apply the finishing touches with a knife, but there is a better tool for creating hair texture. Narrow knife lines can indicate hair, but since they create very little shadow, the individual hairs don't show up well. The little 11/3 gouge is my favorite for this, and it's also ideal for putting in the curving lines of the mustache and the beard.

Make smoothly sweeping lines with the gouge to simulate mustache and eyebrow hair. Come back underneath the beard to give it a deeper undercut, and accentuate the separation between the mustache and the beard with a deep shadow **(PHOTO A)**.

Alternate forward and backward lazy S-lines to create the beard hairs. Straight lines will take away the visual flow of a carving, so try to cut these lines in a spiraling shape, almost like candy cane stripes. Vary the pattern to get a lively look **(PHOTO B)**.

With your right hand, grasp the gouge up near its cutting edge, holding it against your right thumb and gripping it with your right index finger. With your right thumb as a pivot point, use the other fingers of your right hand—opening and closing them—to help direct the tool to the left or right.

Now look over the carving to see that all surfaces and facets are finished to your liking. Go back with the knife to clean up any rough areas, removing little chips of wood that were left behind, and take off any remaining saw marks.

Part of the charm of whittling is the rustic look that comes from the small facets left by the cutting tool. Since you're not sanding anything later, each cut will be a finish cut. To achieve the smooth surface you want and avoid tearout, it's critical to maintain a razor-sharp blade.

Relief Carving: Wildlife

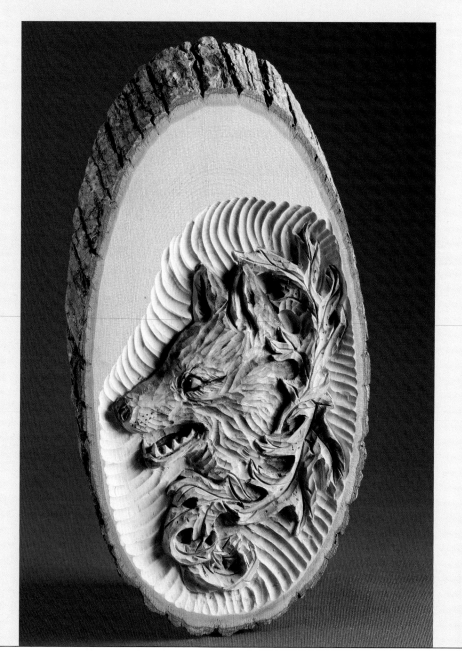

THE TERM "RELIEF" comes from root words that mean "to raise up." In a relief carving, the background is cut away, and the design is incised into the remaining foreground, which effectively raises the image, giving it a three-dimensional character.

Low-relief (or bas-relief) designs are more visibly attached to the background, projecting only slightly. In high-relief carvings, the forms are undercut so they stand out more distinctly, sometimes by several inches.

Many ancient cultures, notably the Egyptians, depicted their ceremonial, religious, and daily lives in relief carvings. Native Americans used the technique to ornament wooden tools and utensils, weapons, masks, boats, and houses. Highly accomplished and strikingly detailed examples of relief wood carvings can be found in churches, palaces, and estates, particularly in Europe, and the practice has been integral in folk-art traditions the world over.

CARVING IN RELIEF IS AN EASY WAY TO experiment and gain confidence in the use of gouges to create three-dimensional modeling. Since you're only carving the top surface, your shapes remain attached to the backing board. You can start with simple designs. As you progress, you'll find an infinite variety of fun and useful ways to incorporate relief carving into plaques, architectural details, and furniture decoration.

Relief carvings of wildlife are a good way to develop familiarity with the wonderfully distinctive curves and visual rhythms of animals and plants, as well as the relationship between two overlapping forms. There are few straight lines in nature, so I find the organic look of a natural slab of basswood well suited as a background for a carving like this, with the bark border as a frame. (Most slabs are cut across the grain, which gives us the bark border as well as end grain to work with.)

Plan your carvings on paper, so that you can work out your ideas before putting tools to wood. That way, you'll know where you're going when you start, and you'll be free to concentrate on technique and on bringing your concept to life.

While whittling can be done sitting down, relief carving requires you to stand. You need a solid workbench that's large enough to allow you to rotate your work and keep tools within easy reach. The bench also needs to be at a comfortable height so you don't have to lean over (protect your back!).

This project will introduce you to the use of gouges. The basic skills you gain as you learn proper cutting techniques with these tools will be the foundation of all the wood carving you do in the future. I also will show you how to use undercutting to create shadows that emphasize the three-dimensional qualities of shapes.

Each piece evolves as I work on it (no change is right or wrong), so the end product does not always turn out as initially designed. You may want to put more leaves in yours or change their shape as you go. Feel free.

USING CREATIVE LICENSE
Compare this photo to the painted fox carving on the opposite page, especially the leaf pattern, and you'll see that even with similar designs, I always allow myself the complete freedom of endless variety and improvisation.

Outline the design

I AM ALWAYS DRAWING IDEAS FOR
possible projects in my sketchbook or on
odd scraps of paper. When I come up with
something I like, I'll usually use tracing
paper to render a final design. That way,
I can adjust the positions of the elements
on the wood to create the most pleasing
composition.

TRACING THE PATTERN Keep a sketch pad with you
so that you can capture ideas and images you stumble
upon unexpectedly. Then use tracing paper to record an
image you want to carve. Tracing paper allows you to
transfer a design to the wood, placing the form artistically
within the frame and changing details as you wish.

1. Once you've traced your design (use a soft-lead
pencil so that the lines are thick), slip carbon paper
between it and the wood **(PHOTO A)**. Position your
pattern so the image creates a compositional balance within your backdrop, and avoid crowding the
bark. Generally speaking, an image slightly off center (in this case, slightly below center) will appear
more lively and interesting.

2. Now go back over your pattern with a pencil to
transfer the image through the carbon paper onto
the wood. The result should look something like the
rendering shown in **PHOTO B** . Clamp the block
down securely. I use a two-part work positioner
(see "Carver's vises" on p. 12) so I can spin the piece
and work at various angles, with easy access to all

sections. A couple of hand clamps also will secure
the work.

3. In broader areas of the design, use a 12/10-mm
V-tool so you can cut the preliminary outline and
remove a fair amount of the background at the same
time. Use the smaller 15/6 V-tool to get into tighter
areas. Rest your left hand on the carving to guide
the tool and prevent it from sliding off your marks
(PHOTO C).

4. Apply steady pressure as you cut a groove
outlining the major elements of the design
(PHOTO D). Work just outside the pencil lines,
leaving them visible.

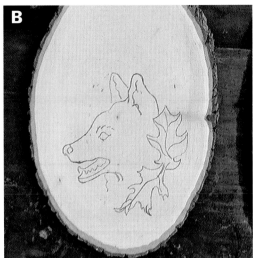

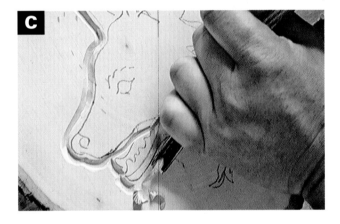

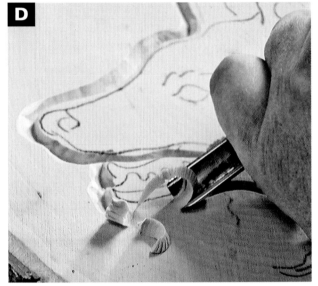

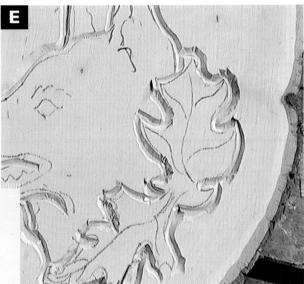

5. Use a shallower cut to outline the edges of the leaves that overlap the fur of the fox, so they appear to be in front of him **(PHOTO E)**. Try to create smoothly curved lines all around, but feel free to change direction as you go into each cut—starting at a leaf tip, sweeping in and around and up to the next tip. Don't be overly concerned about hugging each line with meticulous precision; if you stray slightly, you're just modifying the natural leaf shape a bit.

WORK
SMART

The deeper you cut your outline, the more elevated and dynamic your relief will appear. Sometimes I'll make another pass just to make sure the figures have enough elevation.

Remove the background

1. In many relief carvings, you'll want to remove a lot of background material with minimum effort and still leave wide, decorative grooves. An 8/18 gouge does just that. Start each cut about the same distance to the outside of your outline and scoop down a consistent depth, stopping at the V-cuts **(PHOTO A)**. Keeping the cuts fairly consistent as you work your way around the outside of the design creates a gently spiraling curve along the outer edge of the corrugated background pattern.

CONTROLLING YOUR CUTS To avoid spending excess time removing background material, use the biggest tool possible for the job and adopt a sturdy, wide stance. This stance will help you stabilize your cuts, controlling them as you put pressure behind the tool.

THE CHITTERS

REMOVING THE CHITTERS Even with sharp tools, certain inconsistencies in the wood grain may require you to smooth over chipped fibers that can mar the appearance of your work.

Much of the success of a carving depends on how the cuts look. Frayed and chipped cuts make the whole piece look sloppy.

I refer to those broken, chipped fibers as "the chitters." And you'll find them even on end-grain slabs, because the grain and the density of the wood will vary, since that's how the tree grew.

Harder areas are more difficult to carve smoothly. Sometimes you may need to remove the loose chips, as shown in the photo at left, and go back over some cuts to clean up the chitters, giving your work the look of careful craftsmanship.

2. Start the border at a relatively even width from your pencil outlines as you follow the contours back up along the fox's head, staying away from the bark **(PHOTO B)**. Rotate the carving so that you don't have to stretch to get at different areas.

3. Now go back with the V-tool and recut the outline to get the final depth for the relief **(PHOTO C)**. Use your left thumb as a pivot so you can put the power you need behind the tool. In this second pass along the outline, don't worry about keeping everything crisp and clean. We'll go back and make finish cuts next. Just hog the wood right out, trying to keep the chips you're taking a consistent thickness—about half the depth of the V-tool.

4. Make another final sweep around with the #8 gouge to complete the background **(PHOTO D)**. I put a pencil mark at the top (you'll see it above the fox's ear), so I know where I started. Overlap each cut by about half the width of the gouge, so the cuts are even and the border looks consistently clean and crisp.

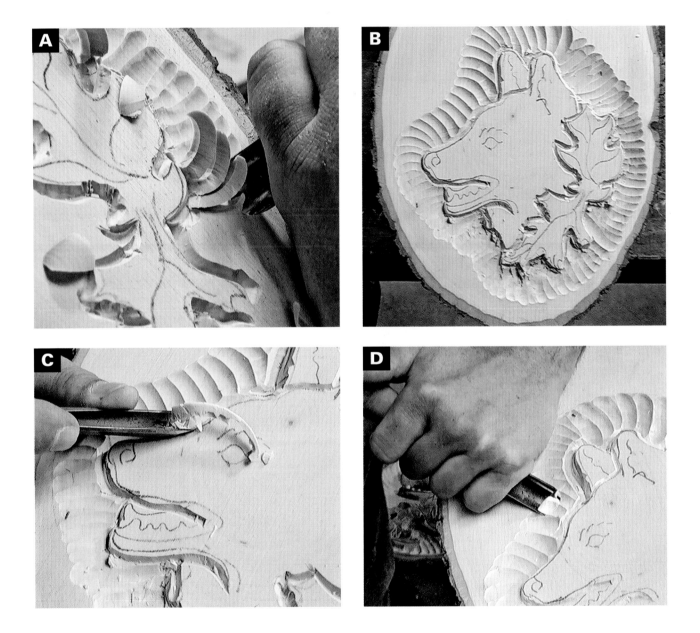

Shape the head

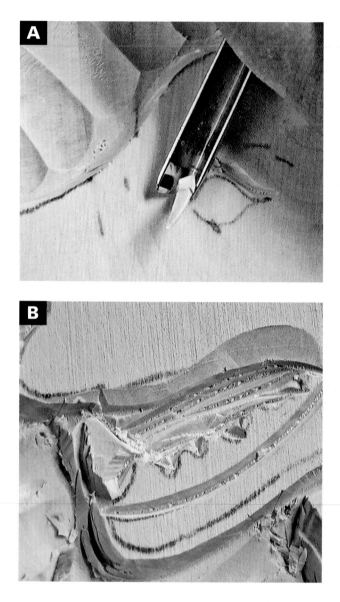

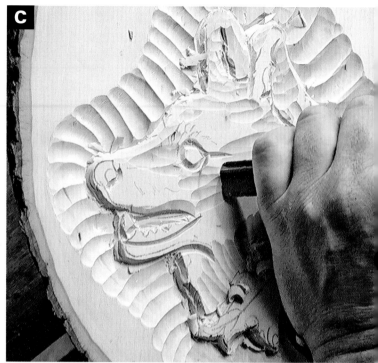

the foreground, they should appear at a higher relief (cut deeper) than the others. Then outline the nostril area of the nose and the curving lines that delineate inner and outer ear elements.

3. Use the 8/18 gouge to round the head and accent major facial elements **(PHOTO C)**. Scoop out some of the inside of the ear to make the cartilage appear closer. The fox's right ear will have to be carved to a lower depth than the left ear because the right one is more in the background, behind the left ear. Shape the contour of the back of the head and the neck as if they disappear behind the leaves. Begin rounding off the forehead, eliminating the hard edge. The forehead resolves smoothly into the eyebrow and the muzzle area.

4. There is a little hollow at the bridge of the nose, next to the fleshy part of the fox's face. This is where the subtleties of the fox's anatomy come into play, to distinguish it from, say, a donkey. Blend the lower jaw into the throat area and begin adding texture to the side of the face.

1. Outline the eye with the narrow 15/6 V-tool, staying outside the pencil line and visualizing the rounded shape you will later want to create **(PHOTO A)**.

2. Outline the lower jaw and remove some of the wood right down to the background **(PHOTO B)**. Then remove some of the wood around the teeth and inside the mouth. Since his front teeth are in

Incorporating spiral curves into the background of a wildlife carving helps lead the viewer's eye into the main subject.

If you look at another version of this fox relief (see p. 46) you'll see I cut the curves to move up and to the right. In the project on these pages, the curves move up and to the left as shown in the photo at left.

In either case, you could imagine the curves represent natural leaves of the fox's habitat.

It's the curve that matters, not the direction; straight or angular lines kill the visual rhythm of a nature piece like this.

WORK SMART

As you work on a carving, keep the total composition in mind. Every detail will affect the overall look of the piece. Develop all the parts in unison, so the whole carving evolves as a single sculpture, not as a collage of different elements.

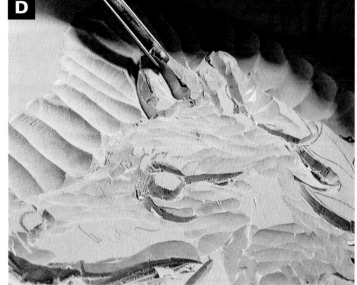

D

5. With the V-tool, put in the little "Cleopatra notch" that extends rearward from the corner of the eye **(PHOTO D)**. The muscle underneath the eye has a fleshiness you can show. The fur on the back of the head and the neck is fluffier and longer than the finer hair on his lips, lower jaw, and nose, so you need to leave a lot of wood on the back of the head and neck to create that fullness when you carve the fox's fur later. You also can refine the ears a bit more with the V-tool. There are three depths you are working with in this little area: his left ear in the foreground, the center of the forehead that runs between the ears, and then the right ear at a lower depth, which attaches behind, on the other side of the head. The ear's interior is defined by a lazy S-curve.

Shape the leaves

CURLED LEAVES HAVE MORE LIFE AND interest than those that are unnaturally flattened. I collect leaves that have blown into bushes and keep those that have the curves and visual rhythm I like to include in my carvings. Such natural samples can inspire you to make artistic decisions about how and where to curl a leaf. You may choose, for example, to wrap one around the back of the fox's head, to tie it into the background.

1. Shape the outside parameters of the leaf and establish the points with some deep cuts right down to the background **(PHOTO A)**. The 11/4 gouge is a deeply curved, narrow tool that will help you get in between the fingers of the leaves, using the curvature of the chisel to help shape the tips. Since this is all end grain, there's little chance of it splitting, so you can really sink the gouge in to elevate the leaf from the background. Redraw or reshape the pencil lines as you go, if it will help.

2. Once they are outlined, you can put some curves into the leaves. (The 11/10 gouge fits perfectly to create surface contours of the leaf, as shown in **PHOTO B**). These animated curves will add impact to the overall dynamic effect of the piece.

3. Soften up the edges. Whereas earlier we were using a lot of power, for these shallow detail cuts, finesse is key. Use the gouge like a pencil, almost drawing the leaf edges with it.

4. We can now go back with the 11/4 to work on smaller details **(PHOTO C)**. At this point, look for any place you might be able to use this gouge, cleaning up rough areas and edges and removing any

USE NATURAL MODELS Having a similar leaf to study while you work helps you understand what the tips of the leaves and the curvature of the veins look like and how the veins are staggered where they meet the central shaft.

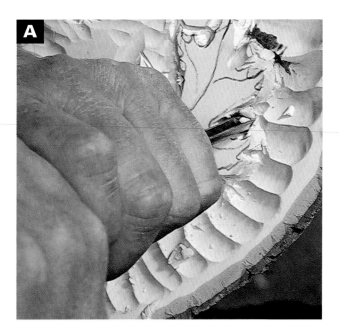

chips. One leaf overlaps the other, so give the upper leaf a crisp edge and recess the underlying one behind it.

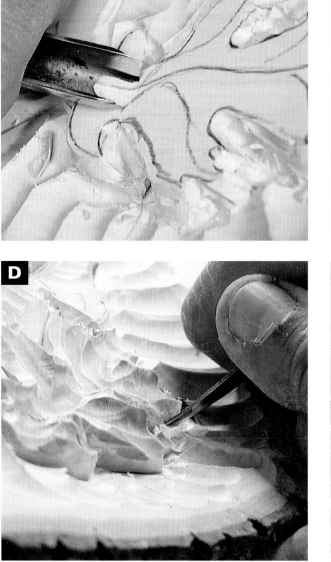

B

C

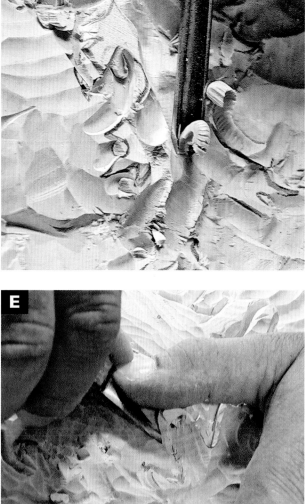

D

E

5. Take off any remaining flat spots on the leaf, as they will show up and look out of place. Use a detail knife to finalize the crisp outlines of the leaves and clean up any ratty edges left by the gouge **(PHOTO D)**. Make deep, curving, angled stop cuts, undercutting the perimeter of the leaves for relief, so the leaf stands out and curls away from the background. Come back and make horizontal cuts to remove the chips and create a clean meeting of two forms and a nice transition where the leaf lays on top of the fox's fur. As you can see, I'm putting quite a lot of torque into this detail blade to create the deep shadows that will give the carving more definition and illusion of depth.

6. I use my left thumb as a fulcrum and guide for the knife, pushing and controlling the cut **(PHOTO E)**. Soften up all the sharp edges.

Refine the features

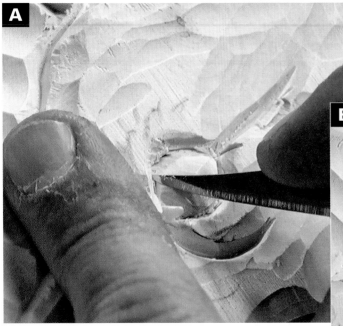

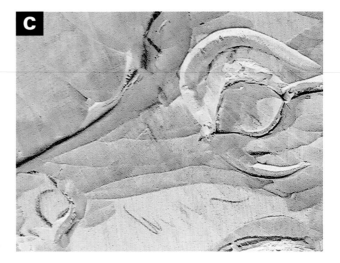

1. Use the detail knife to undercut a deep shadow over the eye **(PHOTO A)**. Round the eye with more of a drop at the front, then soften the back so that the eye looks like it's rolling forward. Lay the blade on its bevel and use it like a spatula to gently shape the wood.

2. Bring the lower eyelid into the tear duct on the inside corner of the eye **(PHOTO B)**. Sketch in an upper eyelid, wide and full, then drop it down into the front corner to give you the illusion that the whole eye is rolling in toward the center of the nose. Use the 11/4 gouge to outline it.

3. Soften up the eyes with finish cuts **(PHOTO C)**.

4. Since the perspective of the image is from a slightly elevated position, the top teeth are hidden by the muzzle. With the 11/4 gouge, remove some of the wood on the inside of the mouth, down to the background depth, following the curve of the

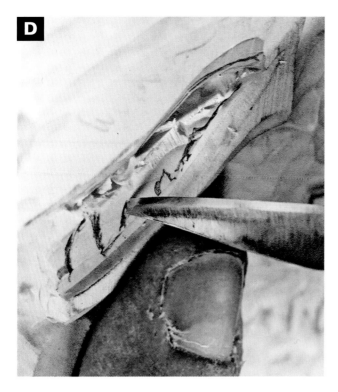

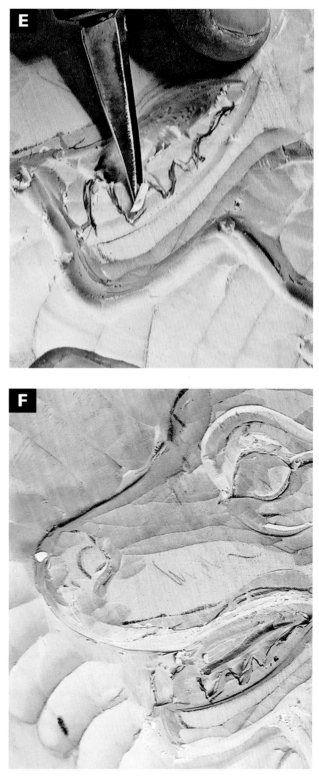

upper muzzle. Shave the level of the teeth down just a little lower than the outside jaw, giving you a new flat surface to draw the teeth on. Sketch them in, then take the detail knife and, holding it on an angle away from the center of the tooth, make stop cuts to outline the teeth (**PHOTO D**). Make all the stop cuts on the left-hand side of each tooth.

5. Then come back and cut away the wood down to the level of the tongue behind the teeth (**PHOTO E**). Make these cuts fairly deep so that you can round the teeth and soften the edges with the knife and the 11/4 gouge. Make sure the teeth start at a deeper level, so that they look like they're inside the jaw. And add the hint of another right canine tooth.

6. With the 11/4 gouge, carve a shadow of an undercut along the roof of the fox's mouth, and outline the top of the tongue rolling along the bottom of his jaw (**PHOTO F**). Backcut the canine a bit, to bring a little shadow behind it and separate it from the background.

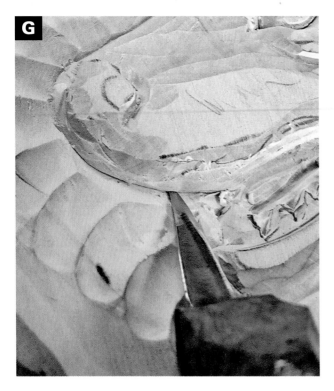

G

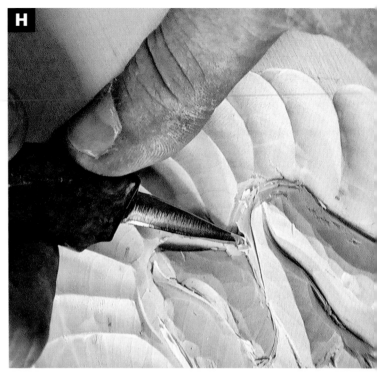

H

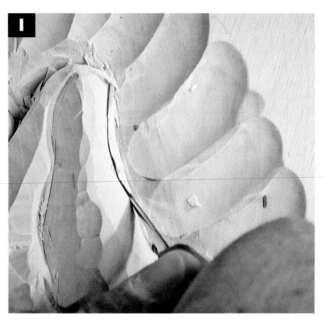

I

7. Cut a stop cut to give definition around the front of the muzzle **(PHOTO G)**.

8. Then finish up the ears. Use the knife to shave and shape the inner and outer contours. Again, leave no flat spots. Now, in order for the left ear to be standing in front of the right ear, make an undercut around the front ear and create a shadow **(PHOTO H)**.

9. Outline the ears with stops cuts and undercuts to remove the chips, creating a three-dimensional look **(PHOTO I)**. The ears should taper down to a point at the tip, with a little cupping midway. So make a few shaving cuts with the #8 gouge to bring the tip to a lower depth than the back side of the ear. Soften any hard edges. Use the #15 V-tool to create a little undercut and shadow for the opening of the ear.

WORK SMART

I generally have one work light positioned to the side so that the shadows help me see the shapes I'm creating. I never light my work directly from above, as overhead light washes out details.

Detail the fur and leaves

BEFORE FINISHING OUT THE FUR OF A wildlife carving, it's helpful to study details specific to the animal. For example, fox fur sweeps up over the head toward the ears. Behind the eyes, it starts to curve downward toward the lower jaw, then wraps around the throat with a kind of swirling, circular motion. The fur is shorter around the muzzle area, and here, too, it has a tendency to change direction with the structure of the fox's skull.

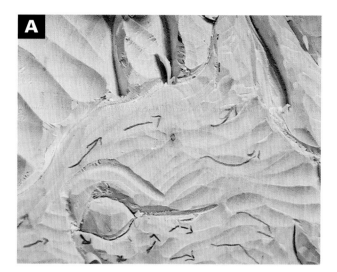

1. Draw arrows to illustrate the natural contours of the fur **(PHOTO A)**. Make curving cuts with the #11 gouge to create the fur texture, with shorter surface strokes around the muzzle, rocking the chisel to get a nice clean cut. Long, coarser hair flows down into the throat so make these cuts a little longer. For the fur on the ears, which goes upward toward the tip, make shallow, short cuts.

2. Texture the inside of the ear. Make a somewhat deep cut with the V-tool to show that the right ear lies behind the outline of the forehead **(PHOTO B)**. Get rid of all the pencil lines and any remaining flat spots.

3. Go back with the #8 gouge and blend the background into the fox's head and the leaves, using very controlled cuts. You don't want to jam the gouge into the finished images **(PHOTO C)**. Use the corner of the tool for little spots you can't get at easily. Any place it won't fit, blend with a knife.

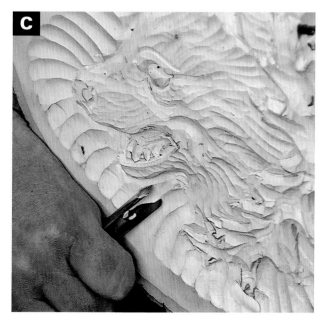

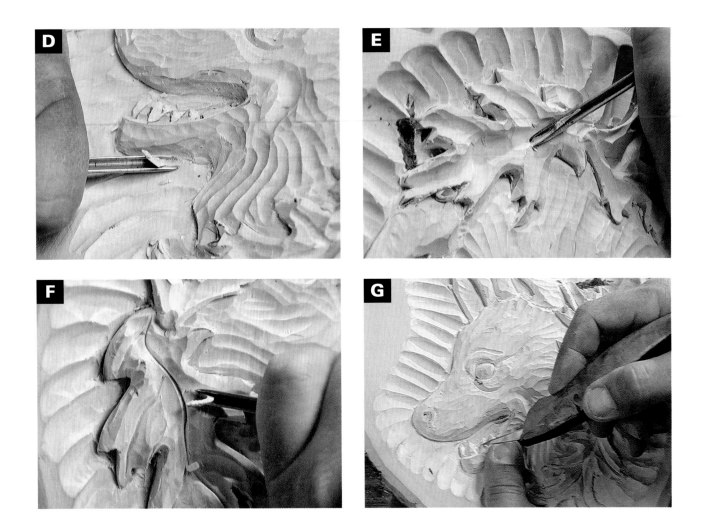

4. Use a 16/3 V-tool to undercut and outline the edges all around and to remove chips **(PHOTO D).**

5. Take the broad 11/10 gouge and thin the insides of the leaves, working in some final curves and twists. Now, using the tightly-angled 16/3 V-tool, carve in the veining you originally sketched **(PHOTO E).**

6. Put in the curving main vein and the staggered secondary veins **(PHOTO F).** While most leaf veins are actually raised, what you are doing is using an incised cut to create simple shadows that give the illusion of veins.

7. Now look the whole carving over. Touch up any final details. Make sure everything is nice and crisp and the shadows are bold enough. Soften up remaining hard edges and get rid of flat spots. Use the detail blade to round things off and clean them up **(PHOTO G).**

WORK SMART

You can never tell what you'll come across inside a block of wood until you cut into it. For example, carving the background of this piece uncovered a small area of ingrown bark. Such eccentricities add to the character of the piece and make each carving unique.

Apply a clear finish

THE DEEP CUTS AND DIFFERENT ELEVATIONS of this relief carving lend themselves equally to staining or painting. Even though I have painted other versions of this fox relief, I'm going to apply a clear finish to this one. A clear stain will bring out the grain of the wood and darken the shadow areas to reveal more depth.

The natural finish I use is Minwax® Natural Stain. You also can apply a darker stain followed by a lighter one, working the darker tone into the deeper recesses to really accentuate the shadows. If I'm adding color, I generally paint with oil stains and use thin washes (see "Painting and Finishing" on p. 168).

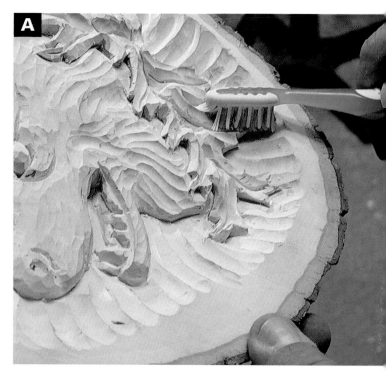

1. Take an old toothbrush and brush out all the little chips that might still be stuck in the crevasses **(PHOTO A)**. You also can cut out a small disk from a Scotch-Brite® pad and attach it to a spindle for a Dremel® or Foredom tool to clean up the work. This technique is a little more aggressive, but it doesn't actually sand the fibers and dull the features. Before you apply the finish, look carefully for any rough places you may have overlooked. Sometimes in a different light or on a different day things you haven't seen before pop out.

2. If you use the Minwax Natural finish, take a hefty paintbrush and swab it on liberally. It soaks right in like a sponge and disappears as you put it on, because this is all end grain. I don't like to cover the bark, as the finish changes its natural appearance. So I stain the surface right up to the edge **(PHOTO B)**. The stain penetrates and seals the wood. It honeys the color nicely and makes the undercuts more prominent, but it doesn't darken the wood too much.

Relief Carving: Landscapes

THIS PROJECT demonstrates another popular type of relief carving: the landscape. The natural areas of the design we'll be using incorporate many of the carving techniques for curving, organic work that we used in the fox carving (pp. 46–61). But the house, with its rectilinear forms, is a good vehicle for learning basic methods for rendering architectural elements such as windows, doors, and siding.

The house also introduces a simple, but strikingly impressive, technique that can really make your relief work stand out—perspective.

A PAINTING OR PHOTOGRAPH

is two-dimensional, and can only suggest depth through shading, sizing, angles, and, primarily, our imagination. But a carving has actual depth, and we can use that, together with those other tricks, to create startlingly realistic dimensionality. In a three-quarter view of the house, the front right corner would be the element that's closest to us. In our carving, it actually is.

In preparation for this design, I took the photo at right of a picturesque old boathouse on a lake, one of my favorite country getaway spots. The broken windows and unhinged doors add to its charm and atmosphere. I framed the shot so the house was off center, a technique I feel can often make a composition far more interesting. When the primary focus of a carving lies dead center in the frame, it seems to do just that—lie dead. In the center.

Then I used my computer to enlarge the photo to the size of my finished carving. When it came to making my design, I changed some details to conform more closely to my romantic image of what the scene should look like. Compare the final carving with the photograph and you'll see I contoured hills behind the scene with almost no vegetation, and I changed the size and shape of the foreground tree substantially. Both of these alterations help draw the viewer's attention to the lines, shapes, and characteristics of the house.

INSTANT RECORD To keep a record of a favorite landscape, nothing beats a camera for capturing the light and ambience you may want to include in your final carving.

Patterns are made to be altered—you could add cows or sheep to this one—geese in the pond, whatever you'd like. Then design a scene of your own next time. Often when you have a personal connection to your subject, you will enjoy carving the work that much more. A landscape relief is a great way to immortalize your property, a favorite location, or some imaginary paradise.

Outline the design

FOR LANDSCAPE RELIEFS, I LIKE TO USE
white pine. It's a smooth-grained softwood that
carves beautifully and is available in wide planks.
For a carving such as this, with a lot of dimensional
perspective, you're eventually going to take the
background down about ⅝ in. total, so you'll need
to start with a board planed to 1 in. thick.

Removing a thick background requires staging
your work. You will first define edges with stop
cuts to a certain depth, then remove background
material with a large gouge, then alternate between
tools, cutting deeper stop cuts and taking away
background until you've reached the proper depth.

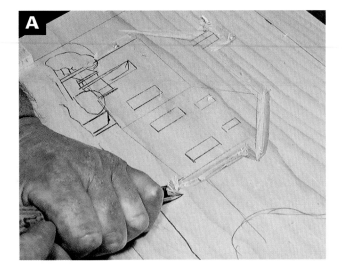

1. Start recessing the background by outlining
the house, shoreline, and tree with a 12/10 V-tool,
staying just outside the pencil lines and keeping
them visible **(PHOTO A)**. Make several passes until
you're almost down the full depth of the tool.

2. Make a shallower cut to outline the bushes and
the stair rails, as they are going to be at a different
level than the house. And run a groove to define
the top of the stone foundation **(PHOTO B)**.

3. Start removing some background with a 7/30
gouge **(PHOTO C)**. This large tool devours wood
so that we can get this grunt work done quickly.
Use a rolling slicing cut and approach the outline
stop cuts carefully. Work from right to left toward
right-facing edges and approach the left side of the
carving from the left. Start just inside the border
and scoop down and across, using a slicing motion
with the gouge.

Transferring your design pattern is not a time-consuming process because you don't have to put in all the lines at first. Just get the main outlines down. The rest will evolve as you carve the work.

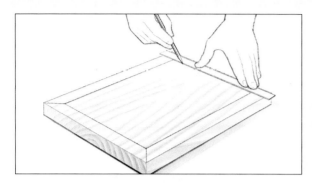

1. I like to run a 1-in. border around the outside to create a frame. Mark off 1 in. all around, and draw in the lines with a ruler.

2. Place your pattern where you want it on the wood and tape it along one edge. This allows you to lift the pattern to make sure you've gotten all the lines you want.

3. Slide carbon paper underneath the picture with the inked side facing the wood.

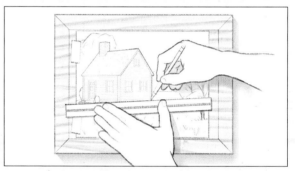

4. Transfer the lines to the wood by tracing over the shapes on the pattern. Use a ruler for straight outlines like walls, windows, railings, and doors, to keep the perspective angles correct.

5. Pull back the photo and check your work periodically to make sure you haven't forgotten to trace any important lines.

6. Then take a thick soft-lead pencil and draw in any additions you want.

CARVING ON TOP OF THE GRAIN

Carving on the top of the growth rings, especially on wide pieces required for landscapes, will prove easier and less prone to chipping and tearout than working from the other side.

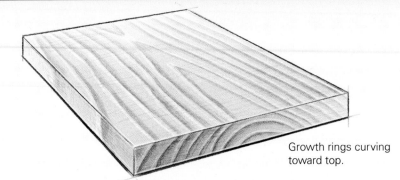

Growth rings curving toward top.

4. Time for another pass with the V-tool—to go down another layer around the outside of the house and tree **(PHOTO D)**. Don't be afraid to work with a lot of controlled power. By leaning into the tool a bit and putting a little weight behind it, you can just bury it right up to the very top. Feel free to widen the grooves; you're just hogging out wood here.

5. Now do a little background removal again with the 7/30 gouge **(PHOTO E)**.

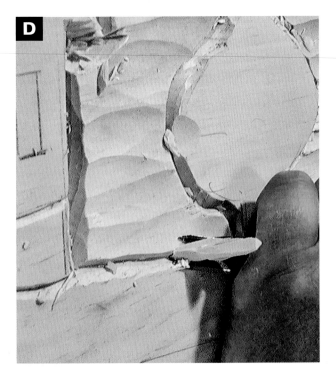

WORK SMART

Even though you're trying to create a flat surface on the background, you should still use a curved gouge. The corners of a flat gouge (or chisel) will dig in and create torn edges.

6. Ease up and use caution around the elevated shapes so you don't accidentally poke into them **(PHOTO F)**. While the perimeter of the house and tree will be cut almost perpendicular to the background, the background should scoop gently down to that point from the level of the border.

7. Try to get the background to a pretty consistent depth of about ⅝ in. You can use a straightedge to check the final depth **(PHOTO G)**.

WORK SMART

This carving won't require a rotating mount. Simply clamp two corners of the workpiece to the table using thin pieces of soft wood to pad the clamps and protect the border.

Put the walls in perspective

TO SHOW PERSPECTIVE IN A CARVING OF a structure like this house, the angles have to taper properly. In this boathouse carving, the central corner where the roof and the two sides intersect will appear closest to the viewer. Penciled arrows on the carving show how all the other surfaces of the house should recede from that central corner.

Since you're going to carve the sides of the house from front to back with a gentle taper, it's best to outline the windows first, so you don't have to go back to square one and redraw them. Since these windows have no moldings or shutters, outlining them is an easy job. Just recess the window openings, carve the walls down to them, and recess them again.

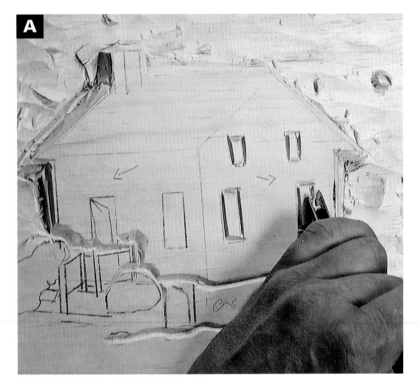

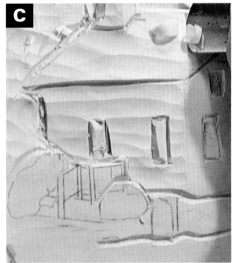

1. Take the 15/6 V-tool and outline the windows on the right side of the house, keeping inside the lines **(PHOTO A)**. Because the windows on the far right will appear farther away, make their outlines deeper than those closer to the foreground.

2. Then, lay the V-tool on its side and use it as a chisel to remove the material inside the window **(PHOTO B)**.

3. Using the same V-tool technique, outline the window and the door on the left (front) side and remove the recesses inside the lines **(PHOTO C)**. Cut the door deeper to make it look like it's broken and hanging open by one hinge. Be careful not to remove the wood you'll need for the rail of the stair landing.

4. Before you put the V-tool down, use it to outline the eave of the roof. Make sure the line above the stone foundation is cut on a gradient that is shallower toward the front and deeper toward the back **(PHOTO D)**.

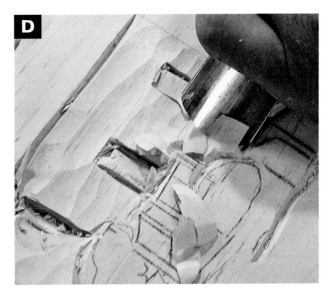

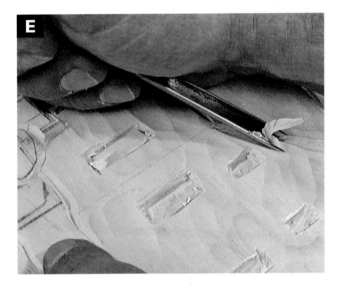

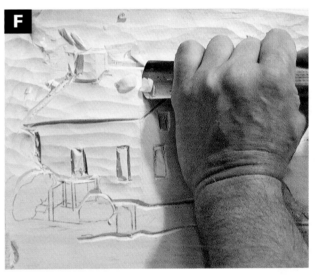

5. Now you can start creating the surfaces of the walls. Use the 7/30 gouge to plane the sides of the building down on a slightly sloping angle, leaving the front corner as the high spot **(PHOTO E)**. Don't go deeper than the stop cuts you made with the V-tool so that you don't lose the door and windows. In tight spots like around the raised railing and bushes, you can use just one flank of the gouge. Then chop down along the lines to remove the chips.

6. Shave the surface of the stone foundation to match the plane of the side of the house. Take the roof down as well **(PHOTO F)**.

WORK SMART

In perspective drawing or carving, "horizontal" lines on the same plane converge to a common point in the distance, called the "vanishing point." If you follow the line across the top of the upper windows on the right side of the house and the line across the bottom of the lower windows, they will eventually meet on the horizon.

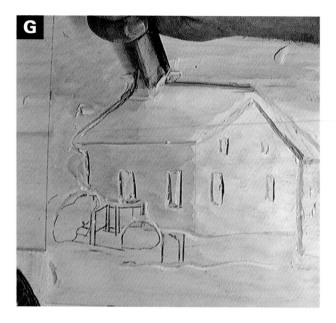

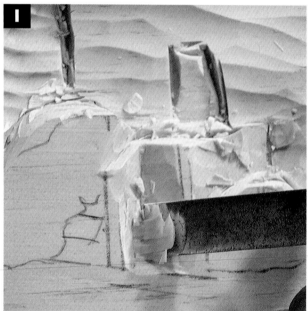

top of the carving, you should see the walls angling smoothly and evenly away from the front corner. Cut in the cellar door quite deeply with the V-tool and use a gouge to scoop out the interior (**PHOTO H**). This door will appear to be hanging open on a broken hinge, also.

9. Notch out the four intersecting planes of the railing with a flatter 3/10-mm gouge (**PHOTO I**). The angle of the two left sides corresponds with the angle of the right side of the house. The front-facing notch corresponds with the front of the house. The angle of the top of the stair railing corresponds with the front roof. And the top of the posts angle just slightly up into the side of the house.

10. Use the small V-tool to lightly outline the bushes and the top of the rail against the house. Then undercut the back eave of the house. The roof has a little overhang that faces the front of the house. Thin down the roof at this point by recutting the outline groove into the background (**PHOTO J**). Put a slight curve right at the end of the roof to show a little warping and to keep things from being too rigidly straight (**PHOTO K**).

7. Carve the sides of the chimney to correspond to the planes of the house. Shave the right side from the top with a careful, swooping cut down and to the right (**PHOTO G**). Remove the chips by carving left across the roof to meet them.

8. Take the walls and roof down almost to the background. If you hold a straightedge across the

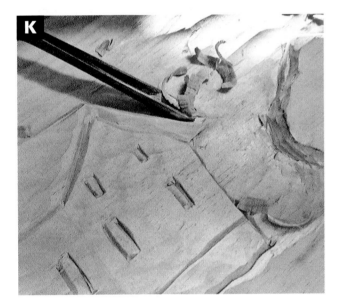

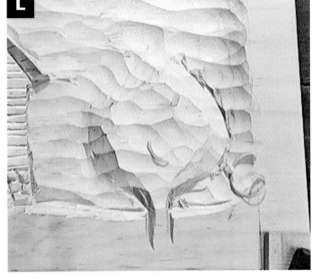

11. Round off the tree with the big 7/30 gouge, blending the tree more softly into the background. Don't worry about the branches and other details yet, just smooth the hard edges. As you shape the tree down from the center, don't stop when you hit the background, but scoop the tool sideways and continue the pass into the background **(PHOTO L)**. Since we made the roofline deeper, you may want to blend the background into it a bit more. Give everything a once-over and clean up any chips or messed up areas before we start to put the details in.

Lay in the windows

1. Check the dimensions of the windows and doors against the pattern with a pair of dividers, and pencil in any errant lines (**PHOTO A**). Lay a ruler across the top and bottom of the windows and correct any lines that are out of perspective.

2. Use a detail knife to cut in the window frames, keeping them consistent with the perspective. The right edge of each window on the sidewall lies parallel to the front wall of the house. To create that same perspective, hold the knife at an angle roughly parallel to the front wall and make deep stop cuts on all four windows (**PHOTO B**).

3. On the left sides of the windows, you can get by with cuts almost straight down because the left sides are practically invisible (**PHOTO C**).

4. Cut the top and bottom sills, then slice all the stop cuts from the opposite sides to remove the chips and create facets (**PHOTO D**).

5. Flatten and smooth the facets created by the back cut, using a 1/6 flat chisel. To create the broken pane in the lower right window, come down

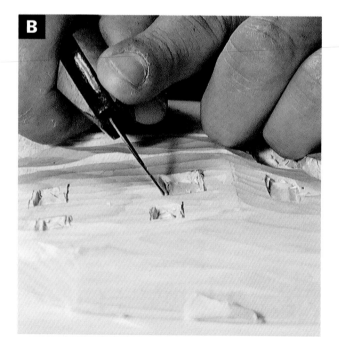

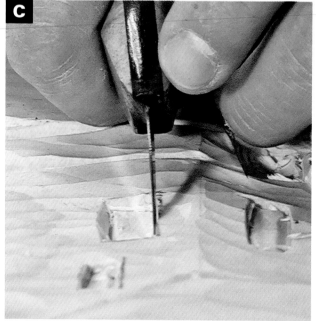

at a deeper angle from the right to create a shadow **(PHOTO E)**. Cut in the window and door edges on the front of the house, using the same techniques, keeping the left edges of these openings parallel to the side of the house and making sure the tops and bottoms line up with side windows. Flatten the pane of the front window parallel with the front of the house.

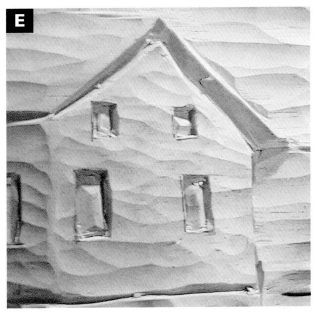

6. To make the door appear to be hanging from loose hinges, make a deep stop cut along its left edge **(PHOTO F)**. This will also form the back edge of the door itself. Make a deep and narrow V-cut at the top of the door, creating a shadow. From the top left edge of the door, cut downward at an almost 45° angle and take out the whole triangular sliver of wood. Use a 3/10 gouge and shave the face of the door angled toward the interior.

Then turn the gouge over and chop down along the right jamb to release the chips. Outline the upper triangle again with the knife and clean out the corner as deeply as you want, as long as you don't come out the back side.

WORK SMART

Spontaneity is a large part of what makes carving fun. In this piece, I changed the tree, and I put a hole in the foundation and roof. What else could create interest? How about hedges, or azaleas, or maybe blueberries? You could add little gardens, a wheelbarrow, geese on the pond, a boat sitting on the shore—all those things would make this carving your very own.

7. Inevitably at this point, the walls will be a little uneven, with highs and lows visible in the widths of the window frames. Use a very wide, almost flat 2/30 gouge to smooth off the walls and take those bumps out **(PHOTO G)**.

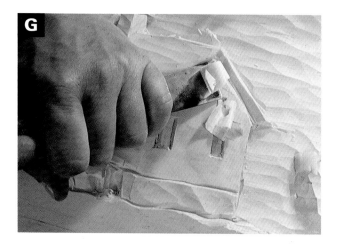

GOUGE MARKS CREATE TEXTURE No need to smooth out the foundation too much; you can use the uneven facets as craggy stone texture.

Carve the siding and shingles

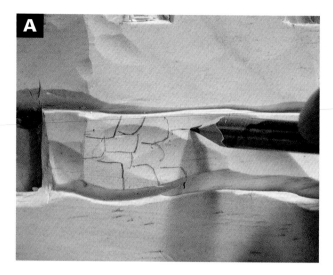

1. Lay out the stonework **(PHOTO A)**. Use a 16/3 V-tool and make straight and curving V-cuts to create a haphazard stonewall. You don't want it to look too regular. Alternate sizes and shapes to suggest the rustic look of an old foundation. Maybe topple one stone a bit; put in a couple of cracks.

2. Every so often make a deep stop cut with the knife and take a little triangular shape out, to break the pattern with shadows **(PHOTO B)**. Make a hole with a missing stone where a raccoon might live. Use the side of the V-tool to take off some of the hard edges from the cornerstones, smoothing the

WORK SMART

You can't get the slicing, rolling motion I advocate for the gouges with a V-tool. A V-cut is more of a straight plowing action. You bear down with pressure, and then roll the tool up and out of the wood to complete the cut. If instead, you come to a stop in your cut and pry the tool up, you'll risk breaking the V-corner of the blade.

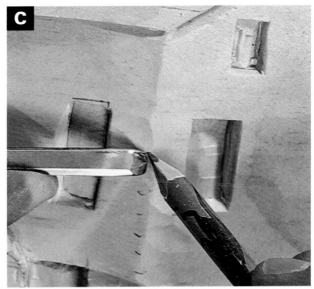

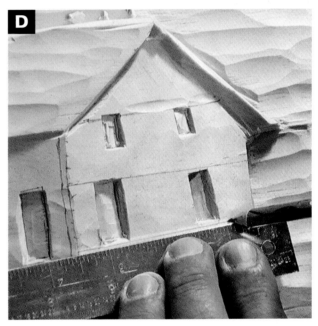

rocks, making them look worn down. Outline some with just the tip of the knife.

3. Lay out the siding. For convenience, base the width of the boards on the width of your 16/3 V-tool **(PHOTO C)**. Mark off the spacing all the way up the side of the house.

4. It's a good idea to have the boards line up with the angle of the window sills, so mark out their perspective lines with a ruler **(PHOTO D)**. Make sure the siding gets a little narrower on the far side. You can adjust the window heights a little if you need to.

LITTLE THINGS ADD UP

I have a philosophy about carving. One little detail doesn't amount to much. But a lot of little things add up to a big thing. If you think about balancing compositional and design details, forms, shapes, and textures, you can establish a connection between elements. They all have a reason and they all contribute to the piece.

The little shadows that we put in, the curvature of the branches (as opposed to straight branches), the hole in the foundation, the hole in the roof—all this attention to detail should produce a harmonious and interesting composition. Each little thing isn't a big deal, but taken together they can kick the whole carving up a notch.

E

5. To create overlapping siding, lay the right side of the V-tool on an angle and follow the pencil lines. Wobbles will make the boards look hand hewn. You can run the non-penciled lines by eye, remembering to diminish the widths slightly as you approach the rear of the house **(PHOTO E)**.

6. V-cut the eave boards under the end of the roof, parallel to the bottom of the roofline. They can be staggered, so you don't need as many as the siding. Finish off the edge of the siding with a corner board—two V-cuts close together **(PHOTO F)**.

F

ADDING TEXTURE

Don't be afraid to experiment with textures. If you don't like how one style looks, it can always be removed. I started to put in a shallow grassy effect on the background pasture, but the effect seemed too busy and I didn't think it worked with the rest of the carving. So I simply got rid of it with a few quick, shallow passes with the big 7/30 gouge. It's the world's greatest eraser.

7. Cut in the siding on the left side of the house as you did for the right (**PHOTO G**).

8. Now carve the roof shingles. Again, use the V-tool as a guide for the width of the shingle rows and cut them just like you cut the siding. No need to be too concerned about whether each line is perfectly straight. To make the hole in the roof (some added charm) draw the opening and bend two rows of shingles down into it. Use the side of the chisel to create the opening and also the ends of the shingles that are falling into the interior of the roof (**PHOTO H**).

9. Make a deep stop cut with the detail knife—really sink it in. Then remove the chips to make a nice deep shadow (**PHOTO I**).

10. Groove out the rows of chimney bricks, too (**PHOTO J**).

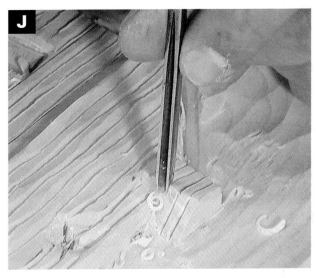

11. Select a width and cut the individual shingles (**PHOTO K**). The lines should run parallel to the ends of the roof. Offset the shingle edges by half a shingle width from row to row. Old split-cedar shingles were all different sizes, so don't worry if you have some a little bigger or smaller. Some can be broken and in need of repair, and the shingles around the hole will be tumbling into it. Then do the same thing with the chimney bricks. Offset the spacing on each successive tier.

Detail the railing and windows

LET'S TACKLE THE RAILING ON THE PORCH. Draw in the corner posts; they're going to be a little higher than the top rails. The inner posts need to be quite close together. Sketch in the stairs, and the bush will cover the other side of the railing.

1. With the detail knife, make slightly angled stop cuts along the sides of the posts and rails to create V-cuts separating the individual boards (**PHOTO A**). Use the very tip of the blade to get into these spots. With your left thumb as a pivot, rock the blade forward so that almost no pressure is being exerted on the knife to create a cut.

2. Angle the stairs back to put them in perspective (**PHOTO B**).

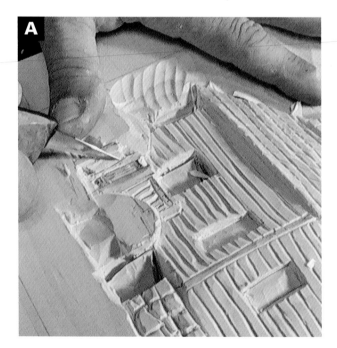

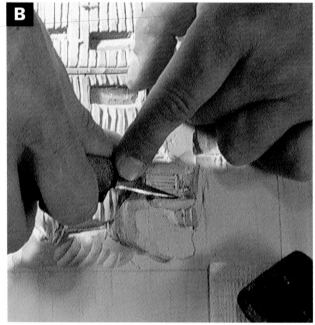

You'll notice that I push the knife, pull it, use it like a pencil, and twirl it around almost like a baton. I put a lot of pressure into it, and I use it very gently.

After you've been carving for a while, you become comfortable controlling the tools and lose the fear that you're going to lop off a finger. Of course you're still careful, but you know the tools so well that the knife or the gouge almost becomes an extension of your hand. You just orchestrate things with it rather than brutally attack the wood. My one limitation is that I cannot carve with my left hand. Some people develop the ability to work equally well with either hand. It is handy to be able to come from either side of a carving. Otherwise, you have to flip the workpiece around to get better access.

3. Make sure the door opening is deep enough, and clean out all the chips **(PHOTO C)**.

4. Clean up any wood chips in the windows, then draw in the mullions **(PHOTO D)**. Offset the center mullion a little to the right in windows on the right side of the house and to the left in windows on the front. Divide the small upper windows in four, but angle half of the broken window on the lower right.

5. Hold the knife at about a 45° angle to avoid fracturing the mullions and outline the sashes with stop cuts **(PHOTO E)**. Make sure they meet at the corners. Then make relieving cuts, and pop the chips out. Don't worry if you bust one of the mullions. It's an old building. I drew in eight panes on the bottom windows, but that's actually kind of tight work; feel free to do six or four.

Before starting this delicate work, test your blade on a spot somewhere in the carving that is not important yet. Make sure the tip of your blade doesn't have a little nick or a dull, rounded spot that would cause it to chew the wood instead of slicing cleanly. Sharpen well if necessary.

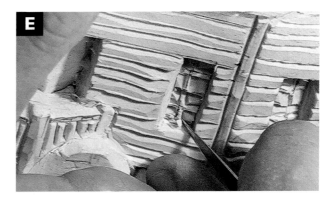

6. Now for the fun window on the bottom right. It's angling into the interior of the house, so you want the sash going in that direction. Put a nice deep shadow where the window and the wall come together, to show the window hanging off by a thread. For control, put your left finger against the side of the blade to steady it, almost like a tool rest **(PHOTO F)**.

7. Detail both of the doors. Take the 3/10 gouge and smooth off the door surface, getting rid of any little chips that still remain. Sketch in the door frames. Use the 16/3 V-tool to put in the details of the cross boards. If you're really good, you could squeeze in a little doorknob, too **(PHOTO G)**. Get rid of any stray pencil lines on the rail with the knife, using shallow shaving cuts **(PHOTO H)**.

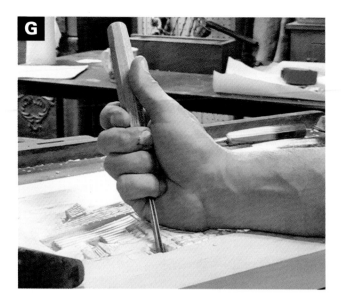

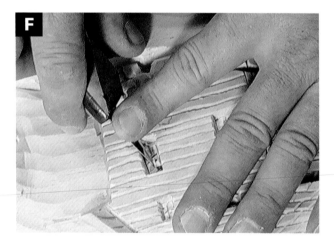

Carve the bushes

DRAW IN THE PRESSURE-TREATED LUMBER wall under the lower bush, and carve in the details with V-cuts. Carve the bushes in three stages, refining them more each time with finer tools. If you want a simpler look, you don't have to take them all the way, but can leave the bushes at any stage of refinement.

1. Use an 11/10 gouge to round over the bushes. Make the cuts radiate out from a central trunk area **(PHOTO A)**. Create a few small haphazard lumps and bumps to simulate the unevenness of a shrub.

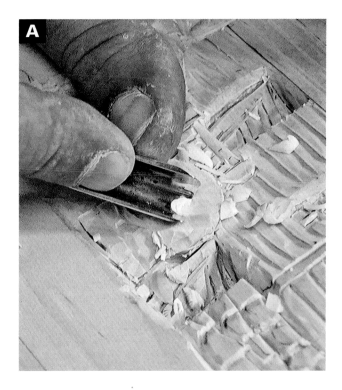

2. Play with a little texturing, to see what you can do with your tools to get the look of foliage. Take a smaller #11 gouge, also called a veiner, in a 4-mm size. Make twisting, swirling cuts, a few to the right and a few to the left, to get a variety of direction for the branches of the little shrubs. This creates an interesting surface contrast to the straight siding-and-roof texture. You can have a couple of branches hanging over the steps.

3. If you want more detail, you could take the little 16/3 V-tool and cut lazy S-curves to simulate some small branches **(PHOTO B)**. You don't need to overdo this step. It just adds a slightly different look and helps familiarize you with the effects you can get using various tools.

Finish the trees and grass

TAKE THE 11/10 GOUGE AND FINISH removing some of the background around the tree, blending into what's going to be the pond. Sketch in smoothly curving branches, rather than straight sticks, to maintain the visual rhythm we've set up with the bushes.

Outline the curves of some of the main branches with the 15/6 V-tool, to raise them into the foreground. Make some a bit deeper, to give

depth to the tree. I also created an opening to lend a more three-dimensional aspect to the tree. Because the tree is a major focal point and takes up a lot of area in this relief carving, you want to generate as much interest in it as possible. Experiment with the hint of a branch going deep and out of view, getting lost in the foliage. Use the side of the tool to soften some of the harder edges and round off the sides of the branches.

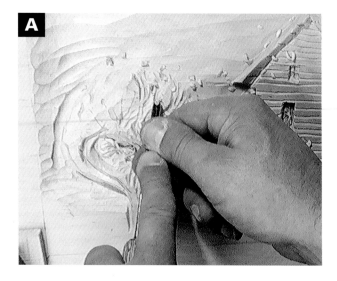

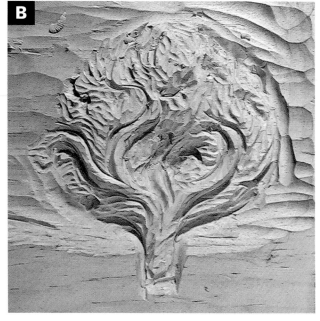

1. Sharpen your 11/4 gouge and create the foliage of the tree **(PHOTO A ABOVE)**. Make little swerving cuts with a flip of the wrist to both the right and left to break up any rigid patterns and to render the leaves more naturally.

2. Every so often—again, not in any specific pattern—put in a few deep gouge marks to create shadows separating some of the branches and to balance the heavier, darker shadows in the building. Round off the trunk with the V-tool, defining its sides **(PHOTO B)**. The grass we'll do next will partly hide the root area.

3. Before we do the grassy knoll, move the clamps so that they are not in the way. With the 11/10 gouge, create wispy cuts to simulate an unkempt lawn **(PHOTO C)**. Angle them so that they sweep off to the right or left, to generate a gentle flow, as though the grass is windblown. Once in a while make a deeper cut to keep the surface from being too regular. Blend the grass around the tree and the building. Then, what's a yard without weeds? Take your 16/3 V-tool and use short curved lines to put in a weed— one of those little additions that don't take a whole lot of effort to create but add another dimension to a carving.

Finish the background

1. You can, of course, compose any kind of background you like. With the V-tool, put in the line for the far shore of the pond and another to delineate a pasture ending in low hills. Then add a line of rolling mountains as a backdrop to your rustic scenario **(PHOTO A BELOW)**.

2. Use the #3 gouge to smooth out the texture of the pond. Clean up the chips around the tree by gently outlining it with the 11/4 gouge in an undulating edge. Don't make a hard defined edge. Clean up any knife marks, chips, or rough cuts in the rest of the background and use a 7/30 gouge to blend and soften any choppy unevenness. Use

shallow slicing cuts from either side to make the background texture disappear into the border inside the frame **(PHOTO B)**. Because the mountains should appear closer than the skyline, level the top background so that it lies just slightly behind the mountains. And just for fun, if you want, put a couple of little birds in the sky.

3. Take a good look at your carving, fixing places you may have missed. Straighten the sides of the house or roof with a detail knife. A few more minutes and a couple of extra cuts here and there can make all the difference in the world.

4. You can finish the border with a variety of treatments, outlining the pencil mark border with a V-tool and squaring it to simulate a frame. You could bevel the edges with a #2 or #3 gouge (or a router). The surface could have a carved or stippled pattern. Or you could simply erase the pencil marks and leave it as is **(PHOTO C)**. But if you want to finish it in oils, see "Oil Painting" on p. 176.

Sign Carving

A HANDCARVED SIGN is the most distinctive, impressive, and personal kind of signage you can have. Whether it's for a business or a home, a handcarved sign says something about you, especially if it's one you've carved yourself.

There is no one magical way to carve signs. The step-by-step directions in this chapter represent the essential techniques I use, though I rarely follow exactly the same strokes each time I do a particular letter.

Sign carving is actually a relatively simple and direct operation. It's also a relaxing and fun activity. The key to mastering it is practice. As you work, you get the feel of how the wood is cutting, and by the time you've finished your first sign, you'll have the hang of this technique and be eager to experiment with others. It's easy to fall in love with sign carving and find yourself avoiding the greeting card shops—everything becomes a handcarved message.

IN THIS PROJECT YOU'LL LEARN HOW

to carve traditional recessed V-cut letters with a knife. (The technique, which employs triangular, well-controlled knife cuts, is similar to the procedure we'll discuss in the chapter on chip carving.) If this were a larger sign, you could rough out the centers of the letters using a router with a V-cutter to save time, and then finish them off by handcutting. But small letters like this cut quickly by hand.

Then, too, simple block letters would be a little easier than those we'll cut for this sign. But I've chosen these letters to help you learn how to make basic curves with your knife (and also because the letters have a bit more charm and panache).

Technique, however, is not the only essential ingredient of successful sign carving. Lettering and the design and balance of the layout are equally important, since they all are elements of a visual composition. The computer revolution has made typesetting easy and quick—you can choose from myriad fonts, size them to suit your project, and print them out yourself. (In the old days, we often used stick-on or rub-on letters and enlarged them with an opaque projector.) If you don't have a computer, perhaps a friend or an office supply store can help you with the typesetting.

A sign is greatly enhanced with the addition of color. We will discuss painting this project in a later chapter. Another elegant, traditional method to embellish lettering is by applying gold or silver leaf. Gold will not tarnish, and if it's applied correctly, it will stand up to outdoor use for years.

The message I've selected for this sign is "live your dream." It bears an accompanying image showing a seed, an opening bud, and a flower. To me, this composition symbolizes planting the seed of a dream, nurturing it to a blossoming bud, and then watching it flower into the beautiful dream you envisioned.

The flower on this sign incorporates relief carving methods we've covered earlier, using gouges and V-tools. It's not an overly detailed flower, but it will add a personal touch to enrich the wording, while the natural curves of the petals will complement the more formal angularity of the lettering. You could choose any design to decorate your sign, from a bunny to the Harley® logo.

ADDING EMBELLISHMENT Both the artistic impact of your design and its message will be enhanced by the addition of details that visually capture the essence of your sign.

Design your sign

I GENERALLY PREFER THE FLUID SHAPE of a circle or an oval for a sign, instead of the rigidity of a square or rectangle. Don't worry about the overall size of the sign at first. Start by experimenting with different fonts and the other elements of your sign. Then choose the size of the board that best accommodates them. If the result is too large or small for the place where you intend to hang the sign, you can size everything up or down as necessary.

I started this design with some lively typefaces whose traditional feel would work well with a V-cut technique. I printed different fonts and cut them apart so I could play with the spacing. The lowercase letters seemed less formal. Then I put my sketches of the flowers in the bottom area, and the layout seemed like it would fit nicely in a 10-in.-wide by 12-in.-high oval. You can choose the shape you wish, of course, but if you're using an oval, see "Making an Oval" on pp. 88–89.

EXPERIMENT WITH LAYOUTS Taking trial runs with sample fonts and decorative elements will help you narrow your design choices. The best one will just seem to fall in place of its own accord.

Transfer the layout

Once you've cut your signboard, you can finalize your layout. Laying out lettering, however, can often be quite a different task than creating a design composed only of pictorial elements.

1. Start with the first letter ("l") an inch from the inside border and adjust everything until you are generally pleased with the overall look **(PHOTO A)**. Notice that if one of your letters creates a wide gap between lines (like the bottom of the "y" and the top of the "d" do here), you can solve the problem by shifting the next line to the right or left.

WORK SMART

Orient the wood grain vertically, so it lies roughly in the same direction as the lengths of the letters. Otherwise, when you cut the vertical lines of the letters, you'll be slicing across the grain and will be more likely to get tearout. It's also usually best to carve on top of the growth rings.

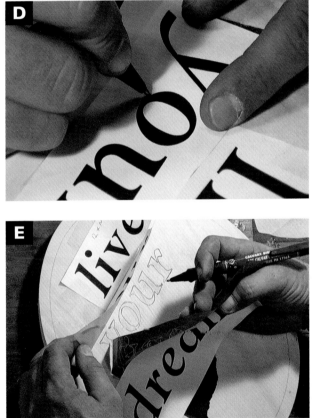

2. I chose to angle the lines to the longest centerline of the board, setting each successive line slightly to the left of the one above it. Once you have arrived at your final layout, tape the letters down along the top edges so that you can lift them up as necessary, and slide carbon paper underneath **(PHOTO B)**.

3. Trace over the letters freehand to transfer them to the wood. Do the tracing methodically, from left to right, to make sure that you get all the elements of the letters **(PHOTO C)**.

4. I use a ballpoint pen because it flows more smoothly. If you need to, you can go back later with a ruler and straighten some of the tops and bottoms **(PHOTO D)**.

5. Check the transfer periodically to see if you've missed any elements **(PHOTO E)**.

Continued on p. 90.

To draw an oval, take a piece of heavy paper larger than the estimated size of your oval and fold it in half lengthwise.

1. Unfold the paper on a board and mark the center point of the fold. To plot the outside parameters of this 12-in. by 10-in. oval, make pencil marks at 6 in. on either side of the center point along the line and at 5 in. above and below the center point. At each centerline end point, mark about a dozen ¼-in. increments **(ILLUSTRATION 1)**. For your first trial run, tap a nail into marks equidistant from each end.

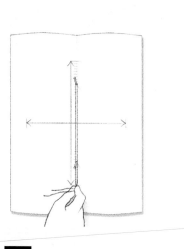

Nails driven at equidistant marks

5 in. 5 in.

12 in.

Center point on fold

Trial markings from edge of oval at ¼-in. increments

2.

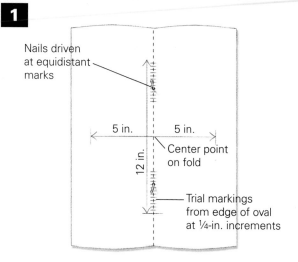

2. Loop a piece of leather sewing cord or heavy button thread (or any thin cord that won't stretch) around both nails and pinch the ends together at one of the 12-in. end points **(ILLUSTRATION 2).**

3. Pull the cord tightly and rotate it around the nails **(ILLUSTRATION 3).** You'll notice the arc will describe the shape of an oval.

4. Adjust the nails until your fingers line up with the width mark of the oval as you swing the cord around **(ILLUSTRATION 4).** Then tie a knot where you were pinching the cord.

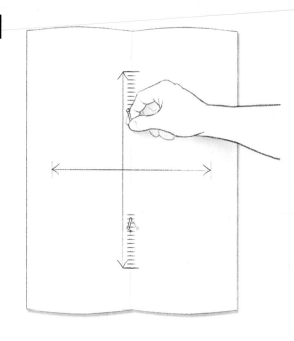

5

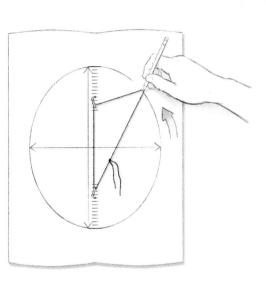

6

7

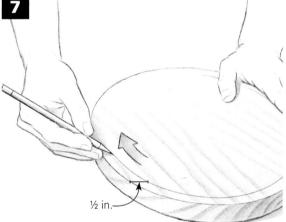

½ in.

5. Slide a pencil point up against the knot, and, while keeping the cord tight and the pencil straight up and down, rotate the pencil around the nails to draw an oval that matches your marks **(ILLUSTRATION 5)**.

6. Lay your letters and flowers out and see how they fit within the oval. If you intend to finish the edge of the sign with a cove (see photo H, p. 90), make sure the layout leaves enough room for that treatment **(ILLUSTRATION 6)**. When you are satisfied that the size will work, cut the paper oval out, and trace its shape on your board.

7. Cut the board with a bandsaw or jigsaw, staying about ¹⁄₁₆ in. outside the pencil line so that you can sand the finished edge. Sand the edge and then, to outline the border, make a mark ½ in. from the outside edge. Hold the pencil on the mark with your thumb and fore-finger, and, while keeping your middle finger against the edge as a guide, run the pencil around the workpiece **(ILLUSTRATION 7)**. This technique is quick and surpris-ingly accurate, and it's widely used by woodworkers and carpenters for many nonprecision markings.

Continued from p. 87.

6. Lay out the flower design. As you can see, I sketched a version of the flower and bud based on a pansy we had in our kitchen **(PHOTO F)**.

7. Select the position of the flowers you think looks best. Here, I flipped the leaf over to the left side of the flower so it didn't crowd the border (that's the handy thing about tracing paper). Transfer the flowers with carbon paper **(PHOTO G)**.

8. Remove the paper templates and check the completeness of the transfer **(PHOTO H)**.

Carve the straight letters

IF YOU USE A WORK POSITIONER OR carver's vise, mount the workpiece and set it up at a comfortable height for carving.

We're going to carve classic V-cut letters, where both sides of the letter meet in a V-shape at the bottom. This is done by making deep, slicing stop cuts all around the penciled outline of the letter, holding the knife at a 45° angle on all cuts—horizontal, vertical, and diagonal—so that they all meet along the center bottom of the letter, and the piece (or pieces) of waste wood just pop out. Here is my procedure to maximize efficiency, precision, and success.

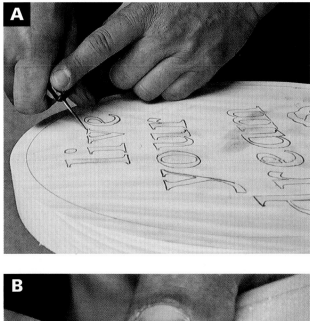

MAKE YOUR WORK COMFORTABLE A work positioner or carver's vise, properly set for a comfortable height, can add hours of enjoyment to your work by reducing fatigue.

1. Cut along the tops and then the bottoms of all the letters in each row **(PHOTO A)**. These cuts function as stop cuts, keeping the action on the sides of the letters (which run with the direction of the grain) from running past the ends of the letters. Keep your knife at a constant angle as you cut the tops and then the bottoms of the letters—except for the hook at the top of each "r," which we'll get to shortly.

2. The dot on the "i" is not going to be a pointed V-cut. Rather, we'll core the dot like you would an apple. Take the tip of the blade and make a circular cut, keeping the blade at a constant angle so that the tip stays in the central part of the dot. And that chip should pop right out **(PHOTO B)**.

Fonts with serifs

The style of type used on this sign employs "serifs," decorative extensions on parts of the letters. Serifs were common on older-style type and served as a decorative and visual separation device that made reading text easier. Because they are thin and delicate, they require special attention when carving lettered signs.

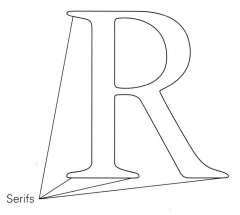

Serifs

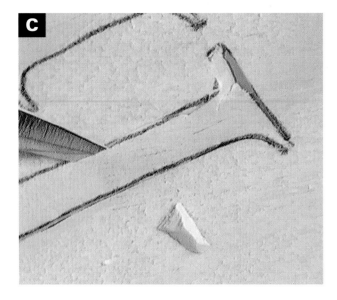

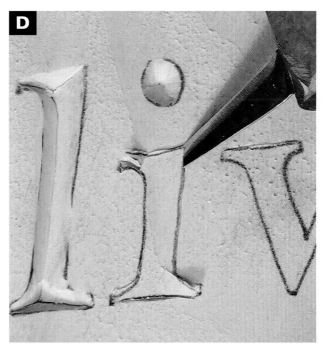

3. This type of font has serifs, the distinctive pointy tips extending the ends of the letters (see "Fonts with serifs," p. 91). Before you finish cutting a letter, make a tiny stop cut across the end of each serif tip with the point of your detail blade. Then slide your knife tip in at that cut and, in a very controlled manner, slice along the outline of the letter, keeping the blade at a 45° angle. Start shallow at the serif tip, and as you come into the curve of the serif, take the knife down to the actual letter depth. Ride the blade along its bevel to get a clean, crisp cut **(PHOTO C)**.

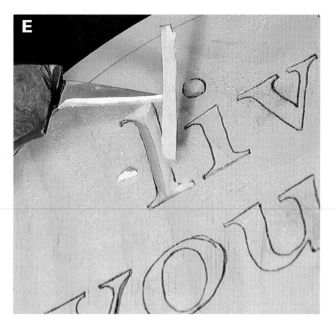

4. Make sure you stop right in the other corner, so you don't overcut **(PHOTO D)**.

5. You're not going to pop every letter out in one whole piece, but some will have a satisfying snap at the end and lift or fly right out **(PHOTO E)**.

6. Come back in with the blade tip and make the upper and lower corners of the letter crisper where the facets meet. It's OK to make the corners a little

WORK SMART

If we had laid this sign out so the grain was going horizontally, all these vertical cuts would be chipping and cracking, and they wouldn't come out as the nice single chips you see in the photos.

deeper (as you see at the bottom of the "l" in the photo C). It just helps accentuate the shadow. Finish cleaning up your serif edge.

7. On the "v," cut the horizontal stop cuts first, then the side edges. It's more efficient to cut the edges that require the same blade angle instead of switching back and forth **(PHOTO F)**.

Carve the curved letters

CURVED LETTERS REQUIRE CAREFUL CUTS. In addition to the curves, you also have gradually varying widths—and thus varying depths. When you come to a fatter part of a letter, sink the cut a little deeper, and then as you start to come to the narrower section, ease your cut to a shallower depth. Try to avoid overcutting. The lowercase "e"s and "a"s are probably the toughest letters to carve.

CURVED-LETTER CUTTING GUIDE

Refer to this guide when carving curved letters. Pay particular attention to the direction of the cuts and make them in the order prescribed.

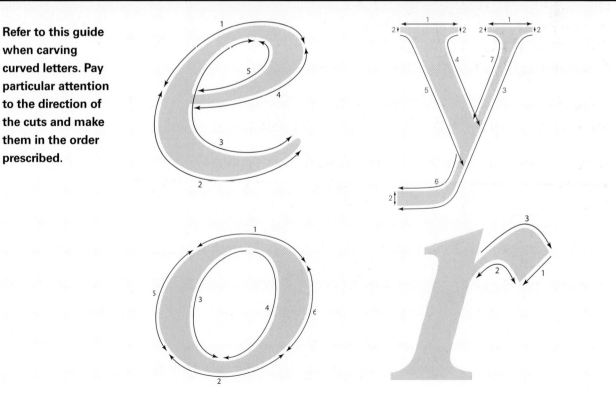

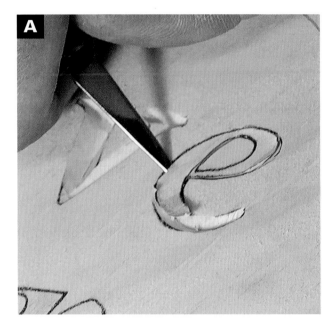

A

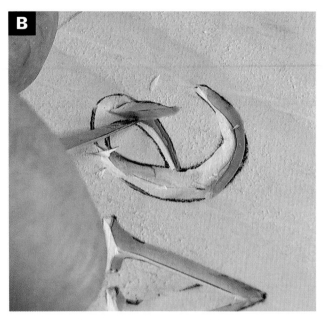

B

C

1. Outline the top and bottom of the "e" first, as you did on the straight letters **(PHOTO A)**. After that, you can probably carve each "e" a little differently, as illustrated on p. 93. The arrows point both ways so it doesn't matter which direction you cut.

2. The angle of your blade, however, does matter. If you're holding it right, you'll avoid popping out the inside teardrop of the "e" **(PHOTO B)**.

3. Go back, if necessary, and make a finish pass **(PHOTO C)**.

4. Starting on the second row, cut out the "y," referring again to the "Curved-letter cutting guide," p. 93, as you make the cuts. Cut the top boundary cuts, then the serif tips and the bottom end of the letter. If the pencil line is a little wobbly, ride the knife on its bevel to help straighten out the cut. Then make the cuts on the left side of the "y," down and all the way across to the pencil line on the far side **(PHOTO D)**. Come back and crisp up the top corner of the V-cut to create a nice shadow. Finish up the other cuts according to the illustration on p. 93.

5. Make the top and bottom limiting cuts on the "o." Cut the inside of the letter, using the illustration as a guide. Again, make sure you angle your blade properly away from the center circle. As you come to the narrower sections, back the knife out and just use a little bit of the tip. You can see in **PHOTO E** that the grain wants to crack and run at the bottom. That's why we put that bottom cut in first; if the wood does splinter, the crack will hit that stop cut and die. Once you've finished the letter, you could put a deeper knife cut along the bottoms of the V-grooves on the sides of the "o." Then, when you paint or stain, the finish will run into that cut at the

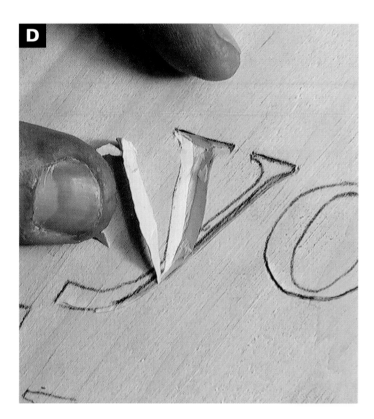

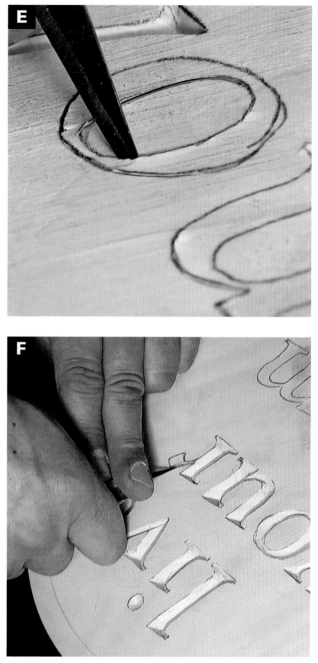

bottom and give more depth to the letter with a strong, dynamic shadow.

6. To cut the "r," first remove the vertical section, just as though it were an "i." The arm is the tricky part of the letter, so you'll want to be careful not to crack it. You could have cut along the straight end of the arm earlier, while you were cutting the ends of the serif tips in the row. Or do it now. Then make curving slice #2 ("Curved-letter cutting guide," p. 93). Come up to the top of the narrow section of cut #3; then with your knifepoint situated in the bottom center of the facet, let the tip stay where it is at the bottom of the V-groove, but swing the rest of the blade right around to the pencil line at the vertical end cut—just the way we did that apple-coring cut on the dot above the "i" **(PHOTO ).**

WORK SMART

If you're using a work positioner, you can turn the workpiece to make curved cuts without taking the knife out of the cut.

7. The chip should pop out, and then you can clean up the bottom of the V-groove with your shadow cut (**PHOTO G**).

8. If a chip doesn't release, you may need to go around and find where you missed a spot or didn't quite connect the cuts. With a thin blade like this, you can slide the knife back in and feel it clunk the bottom where you've already been. Then resume your cut and proceed until you feel the chip let go. After you've finished cutting out all the letters, look everything over and clean up anything you missed (**PHOTO H**).

9. As you turn the piece, the light will play differently off the letters, and the shadows can help you notice places that might need a little touching up—corners that could be crisper, or a serif tip that hasn't popped out yet. But you don't have to be overly worried about getting these things perfect. After all, a handcarved sign should have a handcarved feel (**PHOTO I**).

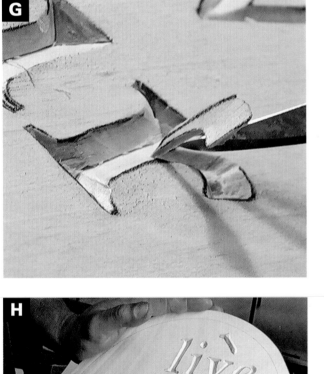

Carve the flowers

1. You can give the flowers a slightly different texture by working with gouges and V-tools. Outline the flowers, leaf, and stems with the 16/3 V-tool. Start with the flower, and wiggle the tool as you cut to create a delicate edge **(PHOTO A)**.

2. Rest your left hand on the carving to act as a tool stop, helping you control your cuts so you don't overrun and have your tool fly past your lines **(PHOTO B)**. You'll want a pretty good depth to the flowers, so that they don't look out of place next to the letters. Use the height of the V-tool as a guide, burying the tool almost up to its top corners.

3. If you go deeper than the tool, its top corners will fracture the outside edges of the cuts you're making, so keep the tips of those corners just out of the wood **(PHOTO C)**.

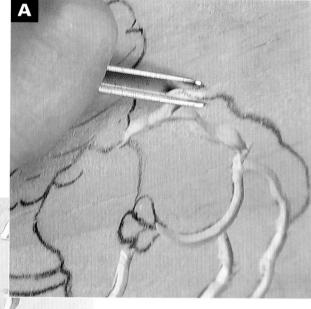

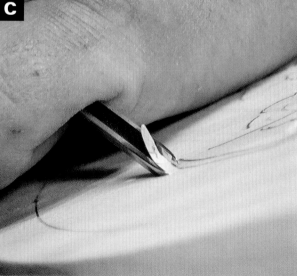

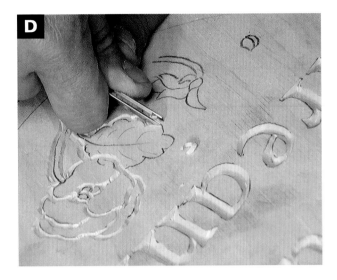

WORK SMART

If you make a slight overcut with the gouge, simply accentuate the curves in the outline with the V-tool to hide the problem. You can see I did this at the tip of the leaf (but don't tell anyone).

4. Make individual little curving cuts around the bumps of the leaf **(PHOTO D)**. Continue outlining the stems, the bud, and the seed.

5. Texture the leaf and flower with the 11/10 gouge. Use curving lines and very lazy S-shapes **(PHOTO E)**. These lines spiral toward the center of the flower like the spokes on a bicycle wheel.

6. Recess the petals in the back a little lower, and, since they tend to curve backward, have the little ripples going into the background. Use the knife whenever you need it to clean up any ratty spots **(PHOTO F)**.

7. Now we can put in some accents with the knife and deepen some areas to produce more dramatic shadows that will help tie this section in with the letters. In the center of the flower, the little triangular shapes represent the stamen and pistils **(PHOTO G)**. We can sharpen the corner shadows in there. To give the leaf and flower more depth, we can get more shadows behind them by undercutting the outline a bit, as we did with the leaves on the fox relief. Also notch in to create a

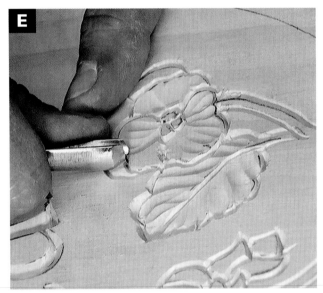

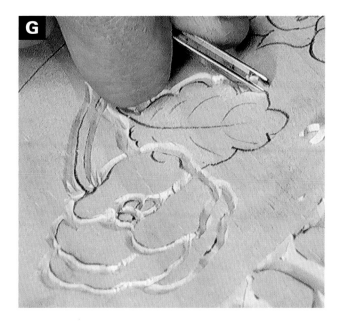

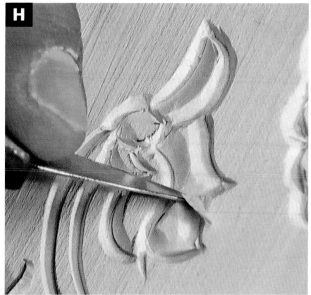

shadow on the back petal, behind the V-shaped indentation of the front petal. If you want to put in some leaf veins, single knife cuts will produce weak shadows that will become more prominent with the application of paint or a natural finish. Pare with

the side of the knife blade to take the sharp edges and corners off the stems and the bud shapes. That will soften their curvature and give them more of an organic feel **(PHOTO H)**. Round off the edges of the seed, as well.

Cove the border

THE LAST PROCESS YOU HAVE LEFT TO DO is to carve the coved border along the outside edge. Use an 11/18 gouge for this cut.

1. Make short, smooth overlapping passes, using a firm, controlled grip and the rolling slicing cut **(PHOTO A)**. Bring the gouge right along the outside of the line, leaving a little wood for the final cleanup pass later. Use the tool as a depth guide; make your passes about half the height of the gouge, and try to keep a fairly constant dimension to your groove. It's critical to pay attention to the grain direction around the outer edge of the oval. It will change direction as you go around the piece.

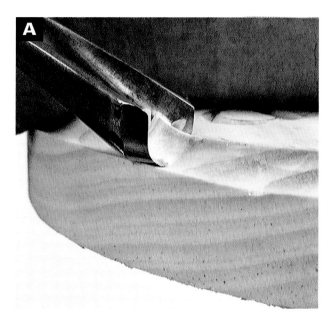

2. You'll need to change the direction you are cutting from so you are always carving with the flow of the grain **(PHOTO B)**.

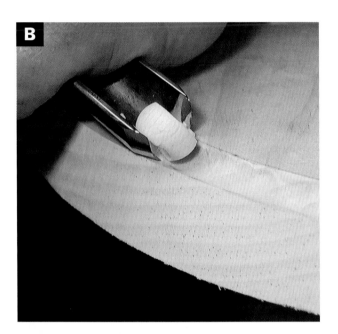

3. Come right up to the grain change before you switch directions **(PHOTO C)**. If you start to go too far, you'll feel the tool dig in and you'll see the cut start to chip out a little. Go further against the grain and the gouge will hook into the grain and split out a hunk of wood. Once you find the going difficult and the chisel starts to catch rather than slice, reverse the direction to maintain a nice clean cut.

4. After you have carved an even cove around the workpiece, do the final pass with longer smoothing cuts. You're just shearing off a thin finish slice right to the pencil line **(PHOTO D)**. Remember to reverse direction as necessary to work with the grain. It's a handcarved border, so don't mind too much if the finished edge has a slight wobble.

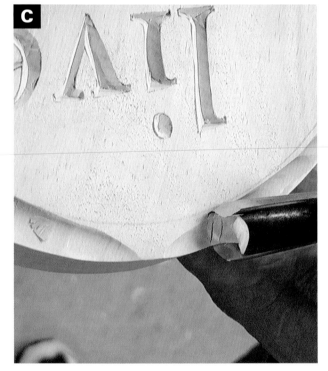

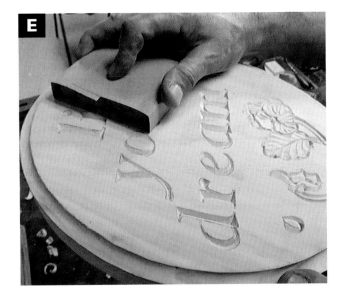

5. Smooth the surface with 220-grit sandpaper wrapped around a sanding block or a flat piece of wood. This removes imperfections on the surface—smudges from the carbon paper, pencil lines, and planer marks—that will show up when you paint or stain. Sand with the grain so that you don't make any cross-grain scratches **(PHOTO E)**.

6. Sand carefully around the flowers—you don't want to take off any of the carved surfaces **(PHOTO F)**. You'll want to have a nice finish on the surface, so be patient and don't rush the sanding.

7. Before you paint or finish your completed sign (see "Painting with acrylics," p. 172), get the dust out of the bottoms of the letters. Brush them with a soft brush, or blow the dust out with compressed air **(PHOTO G)**.

I don't recommend sanding the coved edge. Never underestimate the way different surface textures can add to (or subtract from) the composition of a sign.

Chip Carving

HIP CARVING IS A form of decorative relief that developed long ago across northern Europe. It became an immensely popular technique for decorating wooden objects for the home—from boxes and ladles to chests, furniture, and architectural detailing. For centuries this form of decorative carving remained integral to rural culture. Many of us are familiar with this traditional folk art as it is still practiced in this country by the descendents of German immigrants, the "Pennsylvania Dutch."

At first glance, some examples of chip carving look very intricate and demanding and perhaps even tedious to produce. But actually, chip carving is probably the easiest method to learn, as well as one of the least expensive, because it requires only a couple of knives and some drawing tools. It's supremely useful, since there's no limit to the wealth of functional items you can adorn with designs.

CHIP CARVING IS DONE ON A FLAT
surface with a few basic knife cuts. You will
simply be making angled incisions that meet at the
bottom of the groove, forming a V-shaped facet and
releasing a chip (it's similar to cutting letters on a sign).

Traditional designs generally consist of triangular
cuts that form repeating geometric patterns. Even
the most complex compositions are not difficult to lay
out (regardless of whether or not you have drawing
skills), and the work is satisfying and moves along very
quickly. Very few endeavors in life offer such impressive
results by a beginner who has had just a little practice.

I have set up this chapter to demonstrate how
to lay out common traditional designs as well as
more unusual free-form shapes, and how to make
the associated chip cuts. With a little practice and
imagination, you can expand and combine these
techniques to create your own patterns. Once you
grasp how to make straight and curving incisions
along the lines, it's just a matter of repeating
these simple knife cuts again and again. You
develop a rhythm, and it becomes a meditative
and enjoyable activity.

Because chip carving is so basic and straight-
forward, its successful appearance depends on the
precision and crispness of the cuts. You want to
avoid overcutting, so patience and an extremely sharp
blade tip are key. Chip carving is a great way to practice
knife control.

You can use any smooth, fine-grained carving wood,
but basswood is probably the easiest to chip carve.
Ready-made basswood boxes, like those shown in the
photos, are available at craft and carving supply houses
in many sizes and shapes. Choose what you like to
carve your own designs on.

Many people tell me, "I can't design anything. I
can't draw." That's the beauty of drafting tools. With a
compass, square, and some French curves, you can
produce ornate designs by simply making intersecting
shapes, without drawing one line freehand.

OUTLINING The most fundamen-
tal form of chip carving is outlining a
shape. But as this basswood box lid
demonstrates, even the most basic
skills can create objects of colorful
interest and functional beauty.

Basic outlining

WHILE THIS COLORFUL BOX LID IS NOT A
traditional project, it is a chip-carving project
nonetheless. It's also an excellent beginning exercise.
You'll develop knife control skills that will allow you
to follow a line and avoid overcutting, as well as
maintain a narrow chip cut of fairly uniform width.
Any line drawing or photograph, traced or sketched,
will do. You could even carve your initials. In this
case I chose to draw a South American gliding frog.
You'll outline the image using very narrow V-chips.

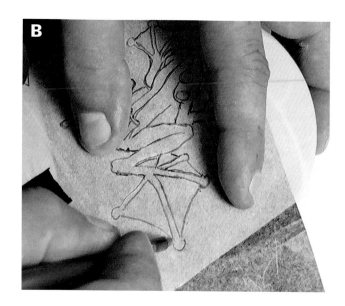

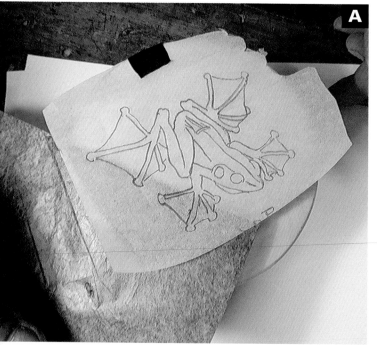

1. Tracing paper is a must for placing such a small
figure on a small background. The paper allows you
to move your image around until you find its best
position. When you've decided where you want it,
tape the pattern in place and slide carbon paper
underneath **(PHOTO A)**.

2. Hold the pattern securely and go over each line
with a ballpoint pen. That way, if you see any lines
without ballpoint inking, you know you've missed
them **(PHOTO B)**.

3. Every now and then lift the drawing to check the
image on the wood, then check it again before you
remove the pattern and carbon paper **(PHOTO C)**.
Carbon-paper ink smudges easily, so exercise a
little care to avoid smearing the lines and leaving
fingerprints behind.

4. Use a detail knife for this project, rather than
a regular chip-carving knife, because a detail knife
will negotiate the small-radius curves easily. It also
will let you keep your cuts tight and close to the

WORK
SMART

> This is a good project for shallow
> relief carving. You would start the
> same way as for a chip-carved
> outline, except that you'd cut deeper
> stop cuts. Then you'd round off the
> body forms and create a shaped
> surface to your carving.

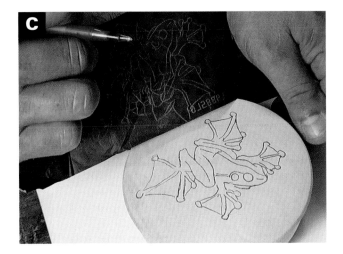

WORK SMART

If you like, for economy of motion, you could go all the way around the frog with one very long stop cut. Then come back and do your secondary cut in the other direction.

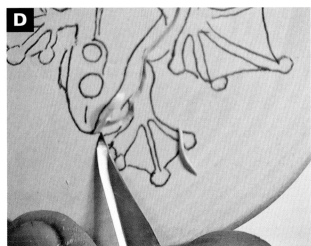

lines. Run just the tip of the blade along one side of the line at a fairly high angle. Then cut along the other side of the line at the opposite angle. When the two cuts meet, you'll produce a narrow chip **(PHOTO D)**. The incisions you are making are referred to as slicing cuts and are the basis of chip carving.

GETTING A GRIP

As you work around the outlines, you'll want to change your grip according to what's most comfortable.

You can cut with a paring or coring motion, using your right thumb to steady and control the cut, as shown in the photo, near right.

Or, hold the knife as you would a pencil, to guide the cut. Very little force is needed. Put your left thumb up against the back of the blade to provide a little pressure to help inch the blade through the wood and also to act as a sort of fulcrum for the forward swing of the blade around the curves.

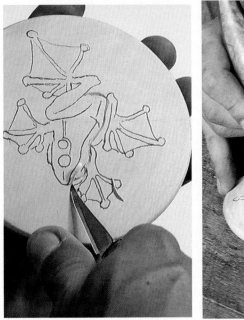

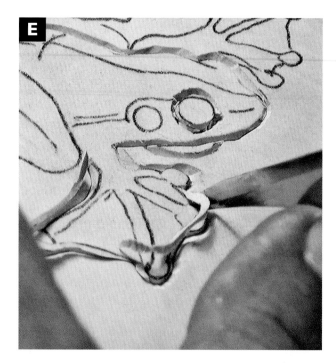

CUT THIN TO THICK

It's important—particularly when you are doing smaller, more intricate cuts—to be aware of where potentially fragile areas are. The pressure of the blade can wedge the wood a little and can fracture the edges of thinner walls. Always make your initial cuts along the edge adjacent to the triangle you've just finished, so that you're cutting away from this thinner wall into the thicker part of the wood.

5. Continue outlining the body and the features. Remember to outline the eye, rather than coring out the center. On the feet, cut more of a vertical stop cut on the line, then cut in at an angle with a long, sweeping cut (**PHOTO E**).

6. Outline the toe bones (**PHOTO F**), maintaining your cuts at a consistent depth. Check everything over to make sure all the lines are complete (**PHOTO G**). See "Carved box lid," p. 170, for decorative alternatives.

Traditional chip-cut borders

THESE TRADITIONAL GEOMETRIC BORDER
designs illustrate the basic triangular wedge-cutting technique of chip carving. Once you master them and the curved versions shown on p. 111, you'll be able to tackle pretty much any chip-carving design you come across, or any that you can come up with yourself.

It's a good idea to try out your cuts on a practice board before you start an actual project. What I've demonstrated are examples of some conventional chip-carving configurations, with the triangles getting progressively smaller. But the possibilities are limited only by your imagination—try diamonds and zigzags, too. The cuts are the same.

Get into a comfortable position for carving, as you're going to be there a while. Some people like to clamp the board down or rest it against a backing block for support. I like to keep it free so that I can rotate it as I work.

1. Orient the board so that the face you're cutting is at the top of the curve of the growth rings (see p. 66). Pencil in your layout as shown in **PHOTO A**. These are ½-in. squares drawn ½ in. from the top of the board, some of the squares with double diagonals and a few with angled lines from the lower corners to the top center.

2. Start with the first square. Lay the knife on about a 45° angle and make a cut into the diagonal line (**PHOTO B**).

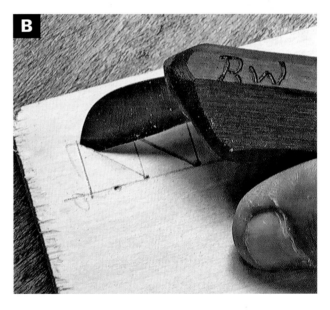

STAYING CONSISTENT

The visual impact of a chip-carved pattern is dependent on consistency. If you vary the angle of the knife, some of your chips will be deeper and some shallower, and the design will look uneven and sloppy.

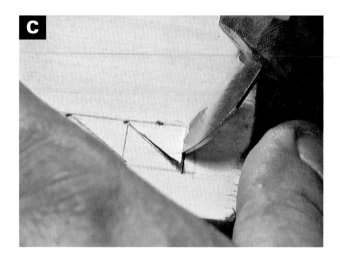

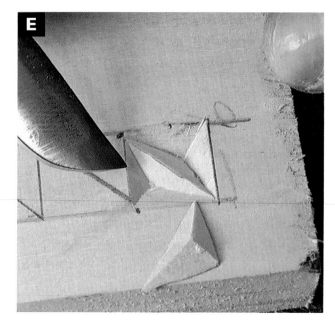

3. Go back to the top left corner again, and,
trying to keep the same angle, make the end cut
(PHOTO C). As you cut along the line, sink the
blade deeper until the tip reaches the center and the
edge reaches the intersecting line. Then draw the tip
out, creating the opposing angle of the V-groove in
the wood. Next, cut along the bottom line, and the
chip should pop out.

4. Move to the triangle on the other half of the
square. Make your first cut along the diagonal, since
this will be the most fragile side. Angle the blade in
the opposite direction from your previous cut, and
slice right at the line so that the diagonal peak will
be pointed. Then cut along the other lines, stopping
where they intersect the border. Then pop the
chip **(PHOTO D)**.

5. Continue cutting out the triangles in the next
couple of squares. You can hold the knife and pull

the blade toward you in a paring cut or push it with
your left thumb as a pivot. If a chip doesn't release
immediately, you may have to go back into the knife
cuts to make sure they intersect. If you don't get a
perfect facet, just go back with the tip of the blade
and clean out any fuzzy areas to make all the walls
crisp and sharp **(PHOTO E)**.

6. Now move to the squares quartered by diagonals
where we have four triangles intersecting **(PHOTO F)**.

WORK SMART

As you lay out patterns, your pencil tip will wear down, causing your line to become fatter. To maintain accuracy and consistency, keep your pencil sharpened or use a mechanical pencil.

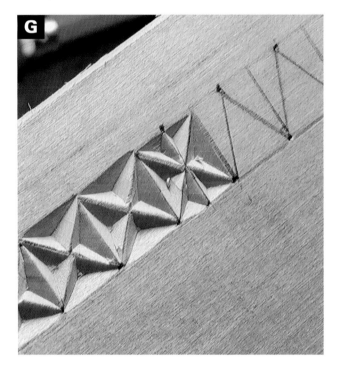

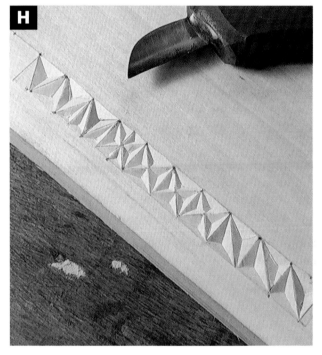

Here you'll use the same cuts, only shorter and a bit shallower. Make your first cuts along the fragile ridges to avoid the tendency of cracking along the grain. You'll get into a rhythm and see the pattern coming together. What you might have thought would be a very complex design, when taken one chip at a time, progresses very smoothly.

7. The next pattern is even smaller. I took the X-pattern we were just doing and sliced it in half.

(If you'd like, you could slice it in half horizontally, too.) Your cuts are going to be shorter and your triangles even tinier. Always think about which direction the angle of the blade should be, so you don't throw off your design **(PHOTO G)**.

8. Now try the six-cut approach on the next few triangles (see "Carving triangular chips," p. 110). You can fill in around them in the same way, or return to the three-cut method, as I did in the example **(PHOTO H)**.

There are two different ways to carve the basic triangular chip: with three slicing cuts or with six cuts—three defining stop cuts and three slicing cuts.

The method I prefer is the more economical three-cut technique. You simply make angled cuts along the lines. It does take some practice to get the angles and depth right, so that they all meet in a crisp, symmetrical facet at the bottom of the groove. Lay the flat part of the blade at an angle to the wood and angle the cutting edge also.

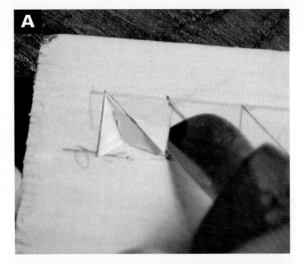

Start shallow with the tip of the blade, and as you get closer to the bottom point of the triangle, sink the knife in progressively deeper until you reach the center of the cut, creating the bottom of the facet. Stop when the cutting edge reaches the line (**PHOTO A**). Then slowly withdraw the blade without changing its angle. After a while, you start getting a feel for the depth you're shooting for, the consistent blade angle, and the amount of force you need to put behind your knife—and your chips start coming out clean and crisp like those gorgeous little specimens shown in **PHOTO B**.

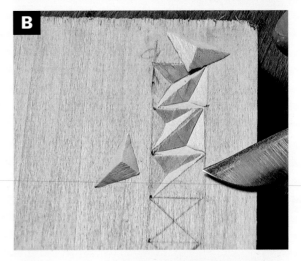

The other method, preferred by some traditionalists, involves making three preliminary vertical cuts into the center of the triangle, to define the bottom corners of the facet. Make the first cut straight down, and stop at about the middle of the triangle. If you bring this line too far, you'll have a conspicuous overcut into the bottom wall of your facet. (If you like, you can draw lines dividing the triangle into thirds first, so you know where the stop cuts are going to intersect.)

Make the other two stop cuts from this center point to the outer corners (**PHOTO C**). Then come in with your angled slicing cuts to remove the three chips, and you'll be able to feel when you reach the stop cuts at the bottom. Many people like the fact that they can get crisper lines at the bottom corners of the triangle this way, since the stop cuts exceed and go deeper than the side cuts, creating little shadows.

Try both techniques and see which you like better.

Rosettes and curves

WORKING WITH CURVES IS WHERE CHIP
carving gets really fun and exciting. Rosettes—
traditional designs within a circle—can be stunning
focal points on a project. You can easily and quickly
create interlocking patterns that are almost mind-
bogglingly complex, simply by spinning circles with
your compass.

French curves can give you free-form creativity
without freehand drawing skills. You also can
incorporate circle or oval templates, as well as cans,
pen tops, or anything else you can find to trace
around to add to your designs. It's best to work out
your designs on paper first. Then you can either
redo them on the wood or transfer them with
carbon paper.

Try the patterns illustrated here, then play
around with the drafting tools and experiment
to invent your own. If you get to the point where
you're really looking for a challenge, you may even
want to pull out an old Spirograph® set. All the cuts
are simply curving and sweeping variations of the
same slicing cuts we did on the linear work.

ARTIST'S TOOLS Just this small collection of drawing
tools can work wonders with a bit of imagination. From
left to right, a collection of various French curves, a
drawing pencil, dividers, a compass, steel ruler, and a
combination square.

PRACTICE BOARD In this photo of another practice
board I was fooling around with, you'll see examples of
some of the diverse effects you can get by altering and
adding more curves and radii.

Carving a six-petaled star

This design results simply from repeated subdivision of a circle into even segments.

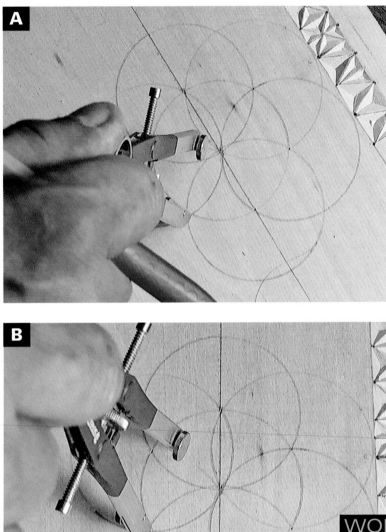

1. Draw a horizontal line with the ruler. Set the compass at 1 in. to give you a 2-in. circle. Place the compass point on the horizontal line and draw the central circle. Then center the compass on each of the two points where this first circle intersects the line, and swing two more circles. Now these three circles intersect each other at four points (two up above and two below) **(PHOTO A)**.

2. Make four more circles, starting at each of the intersections. Try to be accurate in positioning the compass center each time **(PHOTO B)**.

WORK SMART

In a design like this, there are a lot of pencil lines, so you have to be conscious about which line you're cutting and make sure you angle the blade accordingly. But if you do mess up a cut, don't worry about it. Change your design a little. If you mess up at one place, mess up at four other places and it will look like it was the original pattern. Nobody will know.

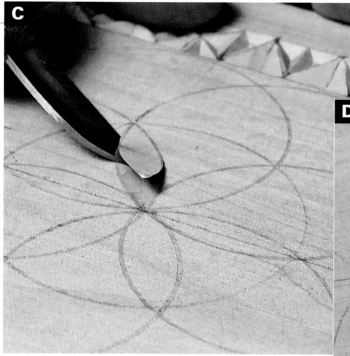

3. Make angled slicing cuts, following the outer contours of the petals. Go a little deeper toward the center, and shallower at the points, keeping the knife at a fairly consistent angle. Let the chip come out **(PHOTO C)**.

4. Repeat this with the rest of the petals. Be careful when you're cutting with the grain so it doesn't run on you **(PHOTO D)**.

5. Since the spaces between petals are wide areas of negative space, lay the knife flatter so you're making a shallower cut. Start along the previously cut ridges, then make the outside perimeter cut—the cuts should all meet so that the chip will come right out **(PHOTO E)**.

In the photo of the practice board (p. 111), the design on the end was carved from this same star-shaped drawing, but I added arcs to connect the tips of the petals, breaking the background into a more interesting pattern. I also experimented, filling in other areas of the intersecting circles with various arcs and curves.

Spiral rosette

This is a very similar design to the rendering of the star, starting with a horizontal line and a central circle.

1. Draw the central circle and the circle to its right (the one with its center at point A, as illustrated in the drawing, lower left. When you make the arc centered on point A, don't go all the way around—start at the upper intersection of the first circle and continue around clockwise until you hit the center of the central circle. You'll see you've created half a petal in the central ring. That's all you're doing with a spiral—only drawing half of each petal. Now position your compass point where the hoops intersect (point B), and draw another circle; then continue around, swinging circles as you did with the star, from each of the points where the previous circle intersected the center one. But don't complete them. Each time, only swing the arc clockwise from the circumference of the previous circle to the center point of the main ring. This should give you a six-spoked spiral as shown in the illustration.

2. Now you have six points where the six outer rings intersect each other (points 1-6 in illustration, lower right). Draw lines connecting these points, running through the center of the main circle but stopping where they intersect the central ring. Set your compass on each of these points (for example, on point C) and swing six more arcs (from points D and E, for example) within the center circle to complete your spiral.

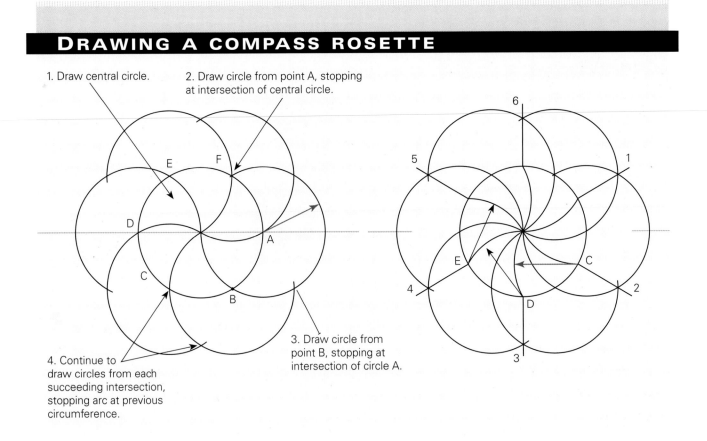

DRAWING A COMPASS ROSETTE

1. Draw central circle.

2. Draw circle from point A, stopping at intersection of central circle.

3. Draw circle from point B, stopping at intersection of circle A.

4. Continue to draw circles from each succeeding intersection, stopping arc at previous circumference.

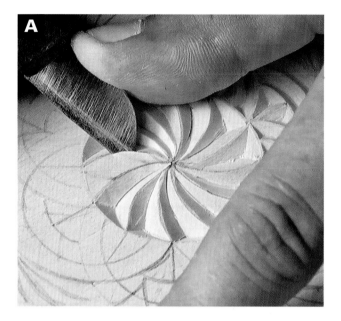

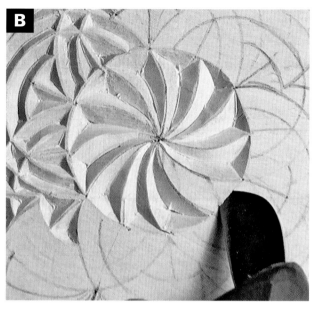

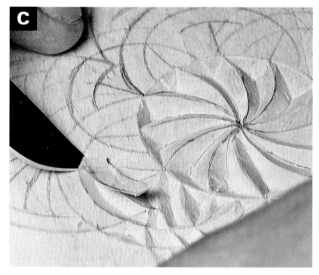

3. To cut the chips out of the spiral, you can make the traditional three vertical stop cuts or just a curving center cut to guide you. Or simply come in with angled slicing cuts, starting at the point and running along the pencil lines, angling the wall inward to the bottom of the groove **(PHOTO A)**.

4. Then make a curved cut along the outer wall to remove the chip **(PHOTO B)**.

5. Carving the other intersecting circles is merely a matter of making the same basic curving V-cuts we've been doing **(PHOTO C)**.

6. To cut the outer rings, swing the inner wall in an outward arc, using your left thumb as a pivot point to get a smooth curve, turning the board as you work. Then cut the ends of the ring. To make the outside perimeter cut, pivot on the thumb of your right hand now, as you walk that hand around the cut, drawing the blade in a continuous arc. The chip should come out just like an orange peel **(PHOTO D)**.

Carving a spiderweb

This design was laid out by centering the compass on the corner of the border and diminishing the size of the radius in ⅜-in. increments. I then marked the outer arc at ⅜-in. increments with my dividers. I repeatedly traced the same section of a French curve from the corner to my marks on the outer arc to get the spiderweb effect. You could also do it with straight lines from the corner. I just happen to like curving lines, and I think they lend a little more interest to a design.

I started carving at the top corner. Since I drew a ½-in. border around the outside of the box, there are only two straight sides to this design. I made the straight cut first, from the radius up to the corner, again angling the blade toward the center of the design. I next cut along the radius, and then made a sweeping cut back up to the corner to release the first chip. All the cuts are pretty standard. On the wide sections the chips can be a little deeper, on the smaller sections they should be shallower.

Cut the fragile walls first to make sure the pressure is going away from them into the thicker wood, to avoid splitting out a wall.

Using French curves and templates

French curves, circle and oval templates, coins, cans, flexible drafting splines, or even bent wire can help you trace free-form curves to add a different dimension to your designs.

1. PHOTO A shows an intricate pattern I worked out on paper with a compass and ruler by layering intersecting and overlapping circles, arcs, and straight lines. I then used a section of the French curve you see in the photo to create curling tails spinning off around the outer edges of the design. These plastic templates are transparent, so you can see where you are laying them on your drawing. Make pencil marks on the French curve itself at the start and end of the section you're using, so that when you repeat the shape it will line up in the same place each time.

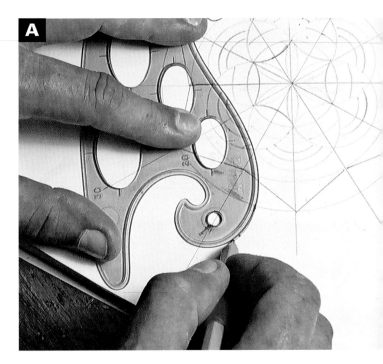

2. To develop this fluid, organic design for a wooden plate I found at a craft store, I used various parts of several French curves to draw petal-like structures emanating from a central point **(PHOTO B)**. I traced around the cap of a pen to get some of the inner curvature I was looking for, and even freehanded a few of the transitions. I also used the oval and circle templates on a French curve to draw swirling, bubble-like shapes around the central forms.

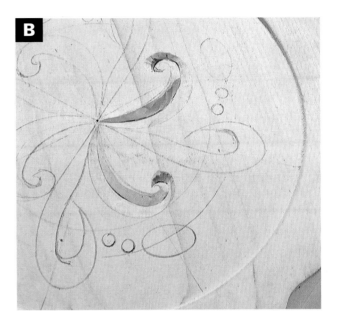

3. Carve delicate forms holding the knife at a fairly shallow angle **(PHOTO C)**. Where there is a very tight radius, it helps to draw in and incise a stop cut down the center, just to make sure you get a nice fluid curve to the bottom. And in a tight turn, where the wide chip-carving knife blade might fracture the wood, use a detail knife's fine, narrow point. To cut out small circles, insert the tip of the detail blade and spin it around as though you were coring an apple, just as we did with the "i" in letter carving (pp. 90–92). And as with that, you get a little conical chip.

Again, if you think you can't draw, think again. Experiment with designs by just placing and arranging different shapes. There are really no wrong designs; there are just poor choices. If you don't like the way something looks, change it. Have some fun and concoct your own designs.

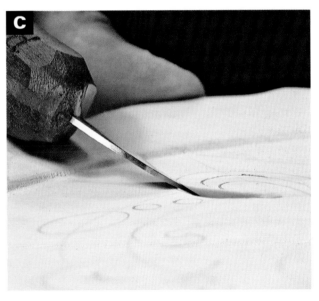

ANYTHING GOES

For the top of the basswood jewelry box, I laid out a design that was a little more intricate to surround the spiral.

I started with the seven intersecting circles. And then I just played around with varying the size of the circles. I left some intersecting, some overlapping, and some intermingling. I used my compass from every which way, with larger and smaller arcs. I even freehanded some curved lines in a couple of the outer circles.

I often make ad hoc templates from any nickel coins—or anything round that suits the purpose at hand.

I've even considered getting rid of the central rosette on a piece like this and having a frog or mouse pop out of the center of the design. Anything goes.

Carving Decoys

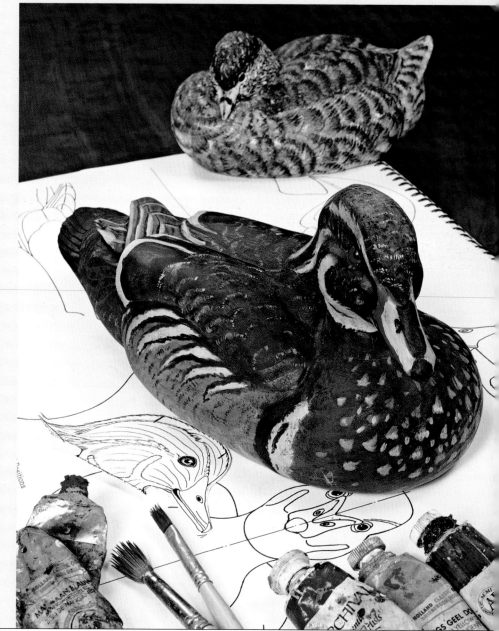

DECOY CARVING started out of necessity—as a way to put food on the table by creating something realistic enough to fool birds in the wild. Many 19th-century Eastern Shore hunters learned to carve their own "duck statues."

As decoy use for luring ducks and geese became more common, carvers began experimenting with likenesses of the more exotic and rare waterfowl. Some craftsmen became extremely skilled as the folk art developed, and it eventually evolved into a full-fledged art form, attracting more than just wild birds. Today, collectors flock to gallery and museum decoy exhibitions and to competitions across the country.

Decoy carving is an extremely popular and satisfying hobby, and it's not as difficult as it may look, for those who are familiar with wood-carving fundamentals. You can find life-size carving patterns on the Internet and at carving shows, and numerous books offer detailed carving and painting instructions.

THE WOOD DUCK WE'LL CARVE IN THIS project is a traditional type of decoy referred to as a hunting slick. This style of decoy was utilitarian in nature, simply shaped without a lot of fragile details—made to be tossed into the bottom of a boat and out onto the river. Hunting slicks are great projects for learning and practicing the basic techniques of decoy carving and painting. Try to find some photos of wood ducks to help you visualize the bird's details and markings as you work.

Commercial patterns will offer multiple views for every type of waterbird imaginable. You can get as specialized as you want—male and female birds, summer and winter plumage, East- and West-Coast varieties. You can make miniature decoys by scaling the plans down on a copier.

Because each duck has subtle differences in head size and shape, posture, markings, and coloration, it always helps to have as much reference material as possible when you begin a carving. I could pick a wood duck out of a lineup, but when I'm carving the bird, I want to make sure I know exactly what it looks like, so I surround myself with photos. You can take a photograph from a book or magazine to a print shop and have the image blown up to the actual size of your final carving.

We're going to do this project in two pieces, carving the head separately from the body. That will reduce the time, work, and frustration involved, and it also will give you the flexibility to shift and select the head direction you prefer, once the carving is near completion.

For this piece I used silky, aromatic dry northern white pine. Basswood and white cedar are also commonly used for decoys. If you don't have a single block of wood thick enough, face-glue two boards for this conventional decorative decoy. (Authentic "floaters" were hollowed out and weighted so they would sit in the water and right themselves when they got knocked over by wind and waves.)

INDIVIDUAL BEAUTIES One of the alluring attractions of decoy carving, or any wildlife carving for that matter, is that no two are alike. Each one has its own beauty and individuality, even when you're replicating work that is your own.

Rough cut the parts

1. Print the patterns full size on heavy paper or card stock. Cut them out with scissors (**PHOTO A**).

2. Orient the board with the curve of the growth rings up. Lay the top-view patterns of the body and head on this surface with the grain running in the direction of the body, front to back, and the centerlines of the patterns parallel to the edge (**PHOTO B**). Trace around the body pattern, but draw a rectangle around the head pattern, since you're going to cut it oversized at this point. Using a bandsaw, cut out the body shape but leave some of the long edge of the board uncut. You'll need that edge when you saw out the side view. Also saw out the rectangular piece around the head pattern.

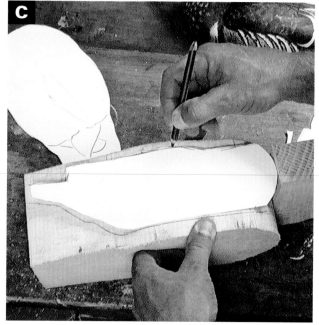

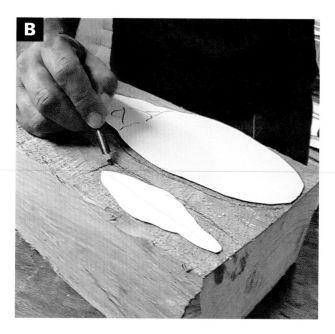

3. Rest the body block on the uncut straight edge and lay the side-view template on the wood, roughly centered across the width of the block. Butt a square block up against the front end of the body block and position the pattern so its front edge touches the square block. Don't curve the front edge down on the contour of the body block. Keep it straight. Outline the side view (**PHOTO C**), keeping the template flat and tracing as much as possible straight down onto the wood (this is easier if you use a thick card-stock template).

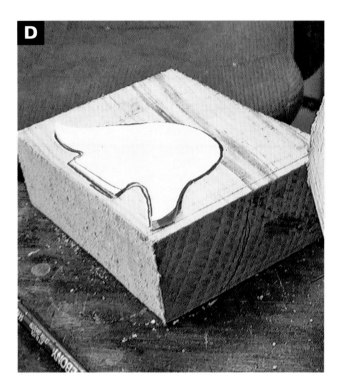

4. Next, trace the side view of the head onto its blank, with the bottom of the neck alongside one straight edge and the end grain of the wood curving up into the pattern **(PHOTO D)**.

5. Now take the body blank back to the bandsaw and cut the contours of the side and the remaining profile of the top view. Then cut the side view of the head, leaving the bottom of the neck flat for support when you bandsaw the top view (which you'll do in a moment). Set the top-view head template on the blank, and, holding it so that it follows the contour of the head, draw its outline. Then saw out the top view **(PHOTO E)**.

6. You may want to knock off some of the corners of the blocks with a rasp, Surform®, or Microplane® so that there will be less wood to carve away, leaving the general shape of the head and body **(PHOTO F)**.

When cutting thick boards, I spray my bandsaw blade with WD-40® first to help minimize friction as the blade slides through the wood.

Carve the body

TO REMOVE WOOD QUICKLY, YOU'RE GOING
to use some fairly large tools. This doesn't mean you
have to whack off huge chips. Keep the tools sharp
and use rolling slicing cuts with a light finesse,
and the work will progress quickly, smoothly, and
accurately.

For this project, I have my Jerry Rig attached
to a portable workbench that is smaller than my
carving bench. That way, I can save a little time
by walking around the work rather than turning it.
This bench has an integral step that I stand on to
stabilize the table (so that I don't end up chasing
the workpiece around the room as I work).

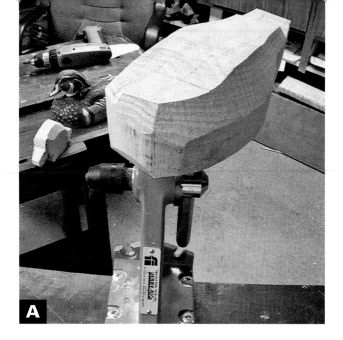

A

1. Screw the bottom of the body blank to a holding
device, work positioner, or wood carver's screw so
that you can turn it and get at the carving from all
angles, as shown in **PHOTO A** .

GOING WITH THE GRAIN

As you're using the wide gouge
to shape the flanks, you are
mainly working with the direction
of the grain. If you look down on
the decoy, however, you'll notice
the sides bow out near the center
of the bird, forming a crest where
the grain falls away in different
directions on either side.

Anything in front of that high
point will have the grain oriented
forward, and behind it, the grain
goes toward the back of the
duck. Make sure you're changing
the direction of your cuts as the
grain changes direction at the
apex of this curve. You don't have
to change the position of your
hands. Just rotate your work
positioner.

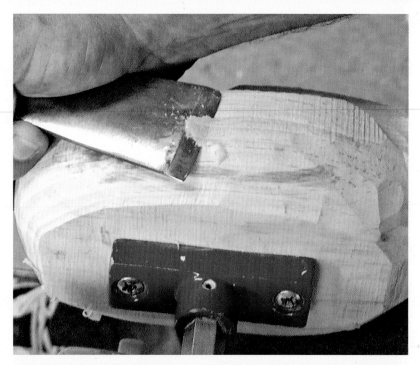

**CHANGE CUT DIRECTION As you work on either side of a point of
changing grain direction, let the feel of the tool and the sound of the work
tell you when you need to change the direction of the cut.**

2. Take a 5/60 gouge, or something similarly low and wide, for roughing out the body in short order. Start rounding the shape of the chest area (**PHOTO B**). What you're doing is hogging away a lot of waste wood, refining the rough shape. You can worry about being delicate later.

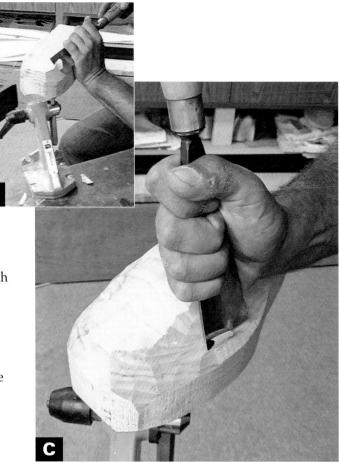

B

3. There is an area on the decoy called the "side pocket." It's the subtle indentation where the wings merge into the upper side of the body. I start that shape with the #5 gouge, using both a downward and sideways motion, slicing with the full width of the blade (**PHOTO C**).

4. Switch to a #11 gouge, in a large 25-mm size. In **PHOTO D** you can see I've started carving in the side pocket with this gouge; I am putting in the Y-shaped separation for the two wings, as well as beginning to taper back the tail.

C

5. Flip the bird over so that you can get at the underside of the tail a little easier. Shape the rump and give the tail a slight curve underneath (**PHOTO E**). The rump area of the duck should be a little narrower than the side flanks.

WORK SMART

You can use a mallet with these big gouges, but gouges actually make quick work out of soft wood like this without mallets. Besides, I find I have more control when holding carving tools with my hands.

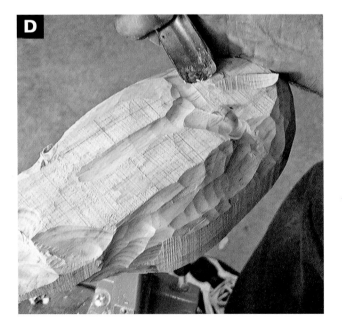

D

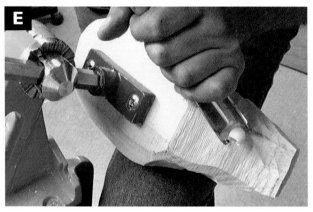

E

In shaping and rounding over the top of a decoy like this, there's a trick that avoids dealing with changing grain direction. Carve sideways across the grain and the wood will cut very consistently, no matter what direction the grain is going.

6. The side pocket curls around the whole flank of the duck. From the pocket down, roll the sides into the bottom of the decoy and get rid of the flat bandsaw marks (**PHOTO F**). Inverting the 5/60 gouge will give you a gentle curve for smoothing and rounding the sides and around the front of the chest area, rather than having a lot of big, choppy gouge cuts on the surface. The area right around where the neck will be joined should be left thick. Once the head is glued on, we can blend the neck and the body together with a smooth flow.

7. Finish shaping and smoothing over the bottom of the tail, blending the side pockets down into the rump. Use the #5 gouge with its curve up or inverted as needed. Round the corners of the tail over somewhat, and create a slight side-to-side scoop under the tip of the tail. Keep a small flat area (left by the bandsaw cut) along the centerline of the underside of the tail (**PHOTO G**).

8. Take a look at the overall carving—check the symmetry, the roundness—look for a nice flow all around (**PHOTO H**). You may want to take it out of your holding device for a better view. Notice that the rise of the wings is not a real high bump.

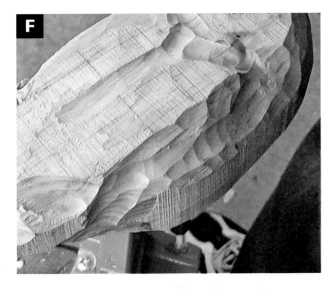

F

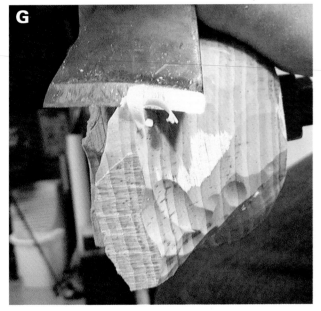

G

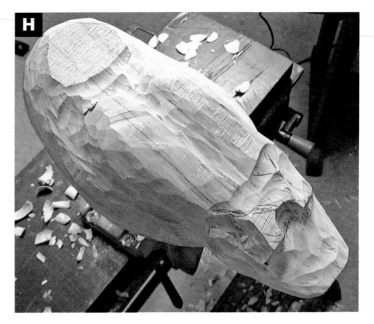

H

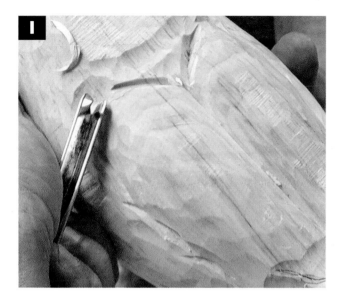

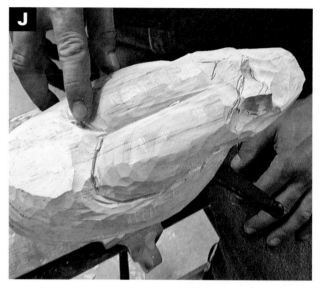

They are more subtle and streamlined curves. Notice, too, the accent in the central pocket between the wings.

9. With a 12/20 V-tool, refine the central groove where the two wings meet, then curl off in both directions to form a "V," outlining the wings folded on the back. You can start by using the side of the V-tool and finish with the flat side (using the tool like a chisel) to soften the corners. Make some wavy, scalloped cuts along the side pockets to simulate the feathering on the flank of the bird **(PHOTO I)**. Continue around and accent the front fold of the wing **(PHOTO J)**.

10. Draw in the ends of the wide back feathers, constantly checking your reference material as you work **(PHOTO K)**. These back feathers are actually called the secondary feathers, and on wood ducks they are prominent, with white edging and a gently rounded end with a slight central point. Then sketch in the outlines of the smaller primaries, crossing over the tail of the decoy. The tips overlap each other and have a slight curve at their rear.

11. Using your pencil lines as a guide, outline these back feathers with the V-tool **(PHOTO L)**. Since this is more of a utilitarian, hunting-style decoy,

we're not going to undercut the primaries and secondaries. Chop down the separation between the two and smooth the tops with the broad 5/60 gouge.

12. Now smooth down their transition into the tail area with a small hollow using the 11/25 gouge, and soften the surface of the tail **(PHOTO M)**. The tail should taper a bit from about halfway back. Use your thumb to press the side of the cutting edge against the wood as you taper the sides of the rump and tail.

13. Step back and take a look at your work on the body; make sure the breast has a nice roll to it. Keep in mind that you still want to keep the transition area where the neck will attach somewhat wide **(PHOTO N)**.

Carve the head

IF YOU LOOK CLOSELY, YOU'LL SEE THAT THE top of the duck's head is narrower than the cheeks. Note, too, that there is a trough that feeds through the eye channel into a hollow in front, and those lines form the forehead and cheek area. The bill comes up very high, almost even with the corner of the eye, and slopes down fairly rapidly. From the front, the forehead tapers down and the beak is quite narrow up at the nasal cavity, widening a bit down where the mouth is. Using your reference material as a guide, be sure to sketch these features in before you start carving.

1. Shape the width of the head from front to back, and then, if you haven't done so already, sketch in the shape of the beak **(PHOTO A)**.

2. There's a lot of wood to remove. Start by using a 11/10 gouge to put in the eye channel that also creates the top of the bill **(PHOTO B)**.

3. Do both sides to keep the face symmetrical **(PHOTO C)**.

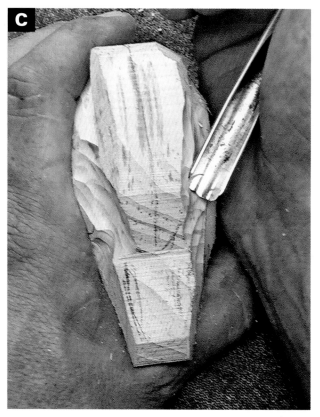

4. Wood ducks have a fairly wide, full, curving crest. Shape this and blend it into the head. You can start to scoop the neck down from the cheek, but leave the bottom fairly wide so we can blend the neck into the chest after we've glued them up. Take some of the heaviness out of the bill, giving it some taper and shape. As you work, keep visually checking the front view and compare the right and left profiles to make sure they're symmetrical **(PHOTO D)**.

CONTROLLING THE BLADE

When you carve small handheld pieces like this duck's head, be very cautious about where your fingers are in relation to the direction of the cutting tool.

With a backhand grip, you can use your back fingers as a tool rest and stop, as shown in **PHOTO A** .

When you carve forehand, rest the gouge against your left thumb as a constant guide. Keep your hands very close to the cutting edge and use a rolling, slicing motion to make a very controlled cut **(PHOTO B)**.

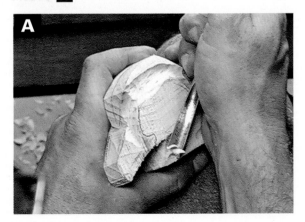

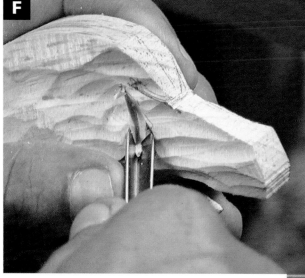

5. The bandsaw usually leaves a rather sharp angle where the underside of the bill meets the neck, so soften that up with a smoother radius. (This would be a tight area to get into if the head were already glued onto the body.) If you look at my finished piece, you'll see there are little bumps on the corners of the bill, with a hollow above, where the bill meets the wider cheeks. Use dividers to check the length and height of the bill on both sides of the face **(PHOTO E)**.

6. With a 15/6 V-tool, delineate the curved edge of the bill as it goes into the cheek **(PHOTO F)**. The forehead dips down toward the center of the bill. Form the distinctive shape of the bill—place the 11/10 gouge right on the V-cut at the cheek, and make a quick twist with the tool as you scoop out the bill's hollow. The pointed bill nail or egg nail protrudes below the tip of a duck's bill to break the hatching eggshell. Shape this and smooth the bill with the detail knife.

7. Thin the upper neck down a bit, and look over the head in anticipation of its imminent union with the body **(PHOTO G)**. Round off the cheeks.

8. Then test-fit the parts to see how the proportions of the head look in comparison to the rest of the body **(PHOTO H)**. The joint between the neck and the chest was a little wobbly on mine, so I flattened the slight hump on the body joint with a wide, flat 2/30 gouge, then touched the two parts on a stationary belt sander to get a truly flat glue joint. A small handplane would work equally well for this task.

9. Position the head until you get an angle that looks natural and relaxed. Put some yellow carpenter's glue on the joint and spread the adhesive with a glue brush or other applicator to make sure it covers the area completely **(PHOTO I)**. Center the neck in the chest.

10. Clamp the parts together and let them sit overnight **(PHOTO J)**.

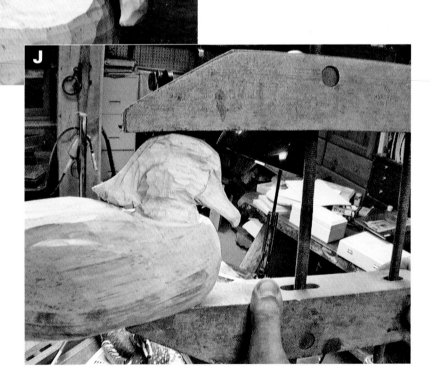

Complete the carving

1. Put the decoy back into the holding device and use the 11/25 gouge to blend the chest and neck joint (**PHOTO A**). What you want to achieve is a smoothly curving transition from the neck into the chest, so your decoy looks as though it was carved out of one piece of wood.

2. Ducks generally have slim necks, so don't be afraid to remove wood. Switch to the smaller 11/10 gouge to get into the tight area underneath the bill (**PHOTO B**).

3. Use that large 5/60 gouge, inverted, to smooth over the hard ridges and soften the whole thing up (**PHOTO C**).

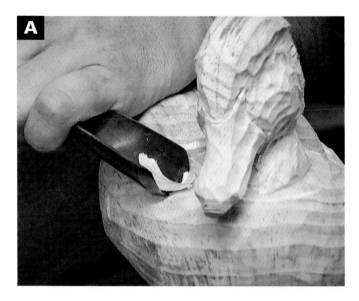

WORK SMART

If you can see a gap in the glue joint between the head and the chest, you can fill it in with wood putty or with glue and sawdust.

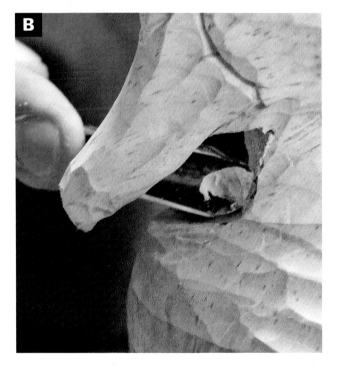

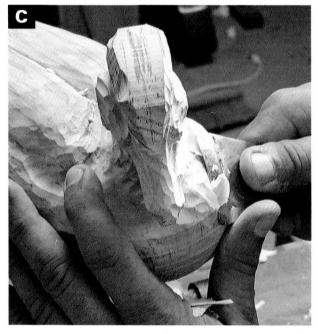

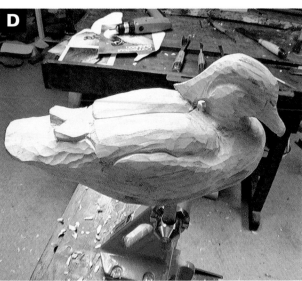

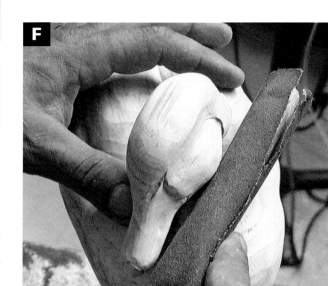

provides a good, solid backing behind the sandpaper and lets you use two hands like you would a rasp to sand the body and smooth the tool marks. Stroke side to side and back and forth in the same stroke **(PHOTO E)**. If you cut the dowel to the same length as the paper, the sandpaper will be right at the ends of the dowel so you can get into some of the tight areas your fingers would get worn and cramped trying to reach.

Every so often, as it gets gunked up, clean the sandpaper by tapping it, or just take it off the dowel and roll it with the other side in, to expose a fresh surface. Substitute a pencil for the dowel to get into narrower areas.

4. Step back once in a while and just look to see how the curves and the flow are coming along. Smooth over the head and get rid of any saw marks. The smoother you get your surfaces, the less sanding they'll need **(PHOTO D)**.

5. Rip a sheet of 60-grit sandpaper in half lengthwise and roll it tightly around a ⅝-in. dowel. This

6. Sand and refine the entire decoy, looking for remaining rough edges and chips that didn't come off **(PHOTO F)**.

7. Then progress to finer papers, finishing with 220 grit and an even, smooth surface **(PHOTO G)**.

Install the eyes

GLASS EYES LOOK QUITE REALISTIC IN animal carvings, and I have amassed a collection of various sizes and types, including some antique taxidermic eyes shown in the photo below. You can purchase them from the suppliers listed in the back of this book. Or you could follow the technique of some of the old-timers and use painted copper tacks, or simply paint the eyes directly onto the decoy.

Glass eyes are available in many colors, though I also often use a clear glass eye with a black pupil, and paint the back with acrylic paint or enamel. Wood ducks have reddish eyes.

Make sure you choose eyes proportional to the size of the head. Each bird is different—here's where your photos come in handy again. The eyes are on wires, so you can bend them against the head to see how they look (see the photo below).

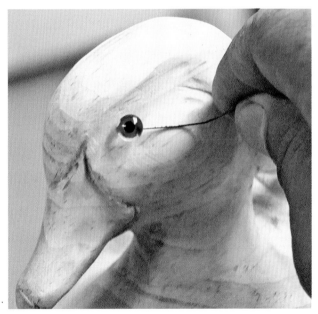

1. Make a pencil line on each of the eye channels. Look straight down both channels from the front to make sure the lines on each side of the face are level with one another. Mark the spot on each line where you want the eye to be. Then use dividers to locate each eye's center point at the same place on each side of the head **(PHOTO A)**.

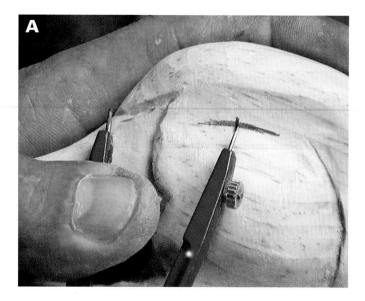

2. Set the dividers to the eye diameter you've chosen and mark both sides of the head at the center points. You're going to epoxy the eyes in place so the hole should be slightly larger than the eye to allow room for the glue to squeeze out and help form an eyelid. I never use a drill for this, because it has a tendency to chip out chunks of the head. Instead, use a small #8 gouge to make a hole about the depth of the eye **(PHOTO B)**.

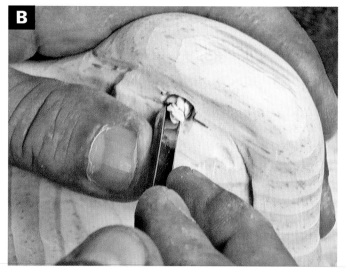

3. Test fit the eyes: They should sit basically even with the level of the forehead, with a tiny bit of room for the epoxy behind them **(PHOTO C)**. If they stick out too far, your carving will look more like a bullfrog than a duck. Take a quick measurement to assure the eye holes are symmetrical. Then clip the wire off the backs of the eyes with wire cutters.

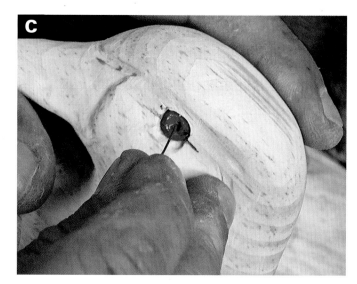

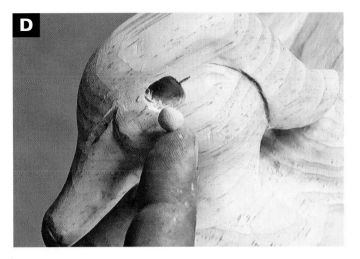

D

4. Slice off a length of two-part ribbon epoxy, and fold and knead it together until it becomes one uniform color. Roll a small amount into a little ball and insert it into the hole **(PHOTO D)**.

5. Place the eyes into the epoxy and squeeze them in. You can see that since I mistakenly cut one hole a little too far forward, I had to widen the other hole so the eyes would sit evenly. I simply took some more epoxy and stuffed it in to fill the cavity **(PHOTO E)**.

6. Flatten and smooth the glue putty around the eyeball, then incise a curving line to form an eyelid ring around the eye. I have an old awl with a knob on the end especially for this task **(PHOTO F)**. Clean any stray epoxy off the eyeball with a knife.

E

WORK SMART

Two-part epoxy is available at carving vendors. The white and blue components mix into a neutral color behind the eye.

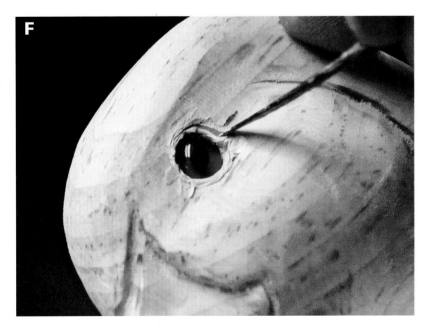

F

Applying gesso and paint

GET OUT ALL THOSE REFERENCE PHOTOS before you start painting a decoy, so you have a good idea of what you are trying to achieve. You'll use acrylic paints, and since you want to create the appearance of an antique decoy, we'll mute the colors by adding a little brown to them. A well-carved decoy deserves a careful paint job. Give yourself ample time to explore the painting and don't rush.

To prepare the base, squirt a blob of white gesso onto your palette and shake in enough talcum powder to make a thick mixture. Blend it until it's well mixed. You don't need to mix up enough to do the entire duck at once—the mix will dry before you're done, so make up more as you need it.

PREPARE FOR PAINTING Lay a wide piece of plastic-coated freezer wrap across your work surface as a palette, and fasten the edges down with duct tape. Have your paints within reach, and a cup of water handy for thinning the paints and rinsing the brushes.

1. Cut off a section of kitchen sponge and use it to dab the mixture liberally all over the decoy **(PHOTO A)**. As the sponge pulls off, it leaves a soft, pebbly texture. If you're not good at sanding or if you got tired of it and left some scratches, this thick coat will cover them up so nobody will ever know.

2. Go right over the glass eyes. You'll clean them later, but smooth the bill now with a paintbrush to remove the pebbly texture **(PHOTO B)**. In places you can't reach with the sponge, use a paintbrush to wiggle the goop in. After the gesso is dry (about half an hour at least), you can start painting.

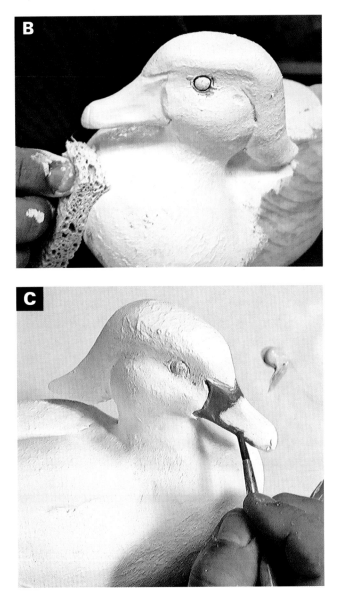

B

C

4. The top of the bill is a dark area. Instead of using the dull black that comes straight out of the tube, I use dioxin purple mixed with some burnt umber to make a rich, warm black. The rest of the undertone of the beak is white. I don't usually use straight white; I use a tan buff and accent certain areas with straight white later. Add a tiny bit of the raw umber to the tan buff and blend it into the neighboring areas so that the bill has a nice antique look. Paint the bottom of the bill a dark brown (burnt umber).

5. The wood duck's head is an iridescent blue green. But to maintain the continuity of the antique and earth-toned colors, I use green with a little brown. With the tip of the brush, stipple in a little of the burnt umber on the forehead. Going back to the reference photos, notice that the cheek is darker than the green on the top of the head and the crest. Take some blue, add a little brown and a little purple, and paint the cheeks **(PHOTO D)**.

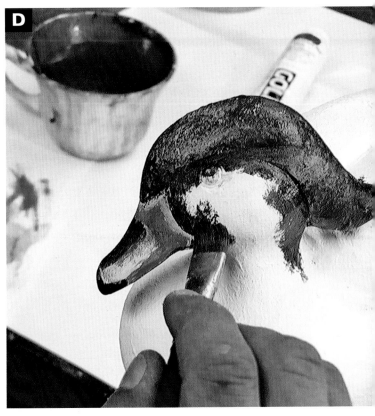

D

3. Raw umber is the brown we'll add to tone the colors down. When you are mixing two colors, squeeze a dab of each separately on the palette and add little bits of the tinting color (in this case, brown) into the other color gradually. Start with the bright yellow, and soften it a little with the brown. Paint the yellow stripe that outlines the back of the bill. Next to that is an orange red that extends across the mandible. Add a little white and some brown to your red paint so it's not a bright orange. Paint up against the previous color, so there's a narrow band left around the bill **(PHOTO C)**.

6. To make the chestnut color of a wood duck's chest, grab some burnt sienna and add a small amount of red and some raw umber. Apply this paint to the chest up to the point about even with where the shoulder ends and the wings go into the body, chest, and the neck area. Stipple a little of that purple on with the tip of the brush to add a sort of feathery look to the decoy (**PHOTO E**). Also use the purple to blend the chestnut into the darker background of the wing area.

7. Where the chest runs into the lower belly, use that buff color and again stipple some of it up into the chestnut color. Then bring some of the chestnut down into the buff color. Mix purple and brown for the back of the duck, maybe with a little blue, somewhat similar to the cheek color. Paint the tops of the wings using swirling, circular brush strokes, to mimic the lay of feathers (**PHOTO F**).

8. The flanks are a mustard yellow. Mix some buff and burnt umber with the yellow, and paint the flanks right up into the dark area on the back. The bottom rump area gets some buff color, with chocolate brown added. Now we're going to do the tail and the primaries. The front of the side flanks of the rump or tail area are a chestnut. Then back to the bluish, burnt-umber purple-black color for the tops of the primaries, the tail coverlets, and the tail. Bring this right up along the sides of the primaries since we didn't undercut them. Paint the underside of the tail dark also.

9. Now that we have the basic color blocks of the duck covered, as soon as they've dried you can put in the white stripes and the vermiculation on the sides. A #2 round brush comes to a nice point for painting the stripes. The first of the "chin straps" starts right behind the eye and curves down to the bottom of the bill. The second stripe runs from the back of the cheek right down under the neck. Get a top view to make sure the stripes on each side of the face line up symmetrically (**PHOTO G**).

10. There are a few wispy stripes on the head that should be painted with short, light, feathery strokes. One rises from the corner of the upper part of the bill almost like an eyebrow. Another goes right along the eye channel and down along the crest, and one more that runs down the back of the crest.

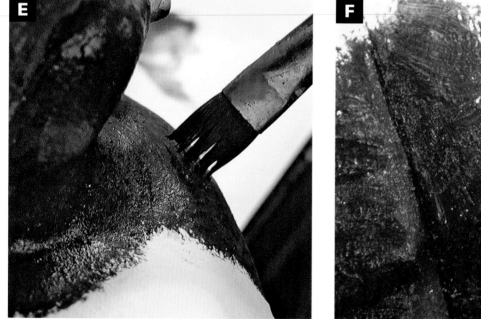

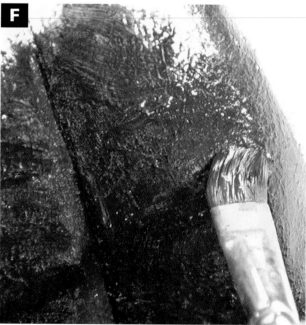

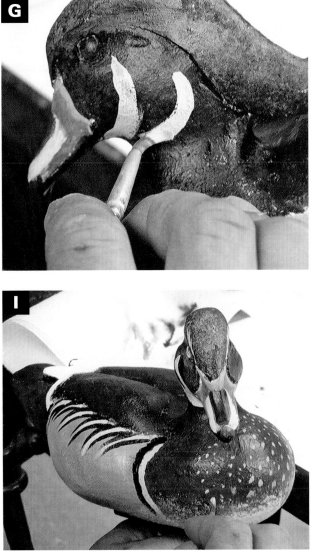

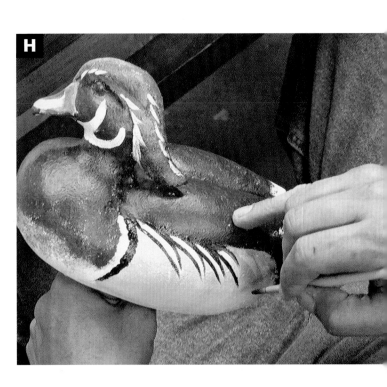

11. There is a curving white stripe that runs between the chest and the side flanks. Wiggle the paintbrush to simulate the unevenness that feathers would have. That is followed by a fairly heavy dark band that's going to go right up against the light one. The white and dark bands just kind of fade away at the bottom. Along the top of the yellow flanks, there are several thin, crescent-shaped white bars with black stripes outlining them, once again fading to a bit of a point **(PHOTO )**.

12. The chest has little white dots on it. Mix a small amount of raw umber into the buff color, and dab in some subtle speckles with a small, round brush. The speckles are numerous and get a little larger down toward the white part of the breast **(PHOTO ▌)**. You can then take a little of the straight buff color and disperse a few sporadic whiter spots for contrast. There's a bluish area along the back of the secondary wing feathers. Mix blue and buff with a touch of raw umber to make a very soft, light grayish blue. Blend this color into the darker color on the back. At the ends of the upper secondary feathers, behind the pale slate blue, put a band of whitish buff. And use the same color to outline the edge separations in the primary feathers.

J

K

L

WORK
SMART

If you mess up when you're painting a detail, don't worry about it. You're using acrylic paint. It will dry in just a few minutes and you can go back, paint over the error, and start again.

13. Take a fan-shaped blender brush and dab its tips lightly into straight raw umber. Gently touch and roll the brush in a few places across the flanks to create the illusion of the wood duck's distinctive feathery vermiculations. I call this light dancing technique "dry brushing" **(PHOTO J)**.

14. When the paint on the duck is dry, you can antique it with a lightly tinted top coat to tone down the colors and give the bird an aged look. Since we're using the oil-based clear Minwax Natural finish, we'll have to use oil paint to tint it. Squeeze a dab of burnt umber oil paint onto the palette, and pour a little of the Minwax into a small dish. Wet a flat, medium-size oil-painting brush with the clear finish and mix some paint into it. Coat the entire decoy and let it cure for a few minutes **(PHOTO K)**.

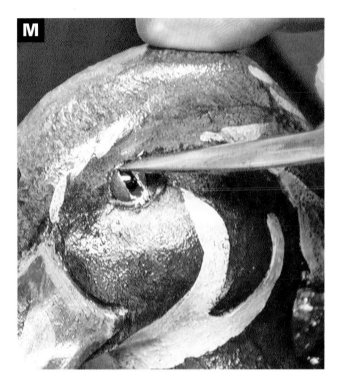

15. Then take a rag and dab it off. Don't remove all of the finish. Just dab off the excess so that the whole thing retains a warm look **(PHOTO L)**. Let it dry according to the directions on the Minwax can.

16. The last step is to scrape the gesso off the eyes with a detail knife **(PHOTO M)**. After you scrape the eyes, the gesso, because of its thickness, may leave a little white ring. Since we've already put the oil stain on, we can't go back and use acrylic paints again. So touch up the eye with some straight mars black oil paint on a little detail brush.

17. The clear top coat leaves quite a shine on the surface. If you don't like this, you can spray the project with a dull (matte) finish. Or you could rub some butcher's wax on to take some of the shine away **(PHOTO N)**.

Power Carving and Woodburning

THE NATURAL WORLD has been the central source of inspiration for artists, sculptors, and carvers since the first cave drawings eons ago. Wood, being a living material and readily carved, is the perfect medium for three-dimensional representations of wildlife.

Grinling Gibbons, considered one of the finest wood-carvers who ever lived, built his reputation in the cathedrals, palaces, and country homes of 17th- and 18th-century England. His exquisite renderings of plants and animals were so fine that a carved pot of flowers displayed outside his home was said to tremble with the vibration of passing coaches.

I designed this small rabbit sitting on some leaves as a wildlife project that demonstrates the versatility of power tools. He's got a relaxed pose, with an upturned back foot scratching his cheek. The power tools are great for creating carvings that mimic the fur of the rabbit and the contoured texture of curled leaves.

UP TO THIS POINT, THE PROJECTS WE have been carving have involved knives and gouges—the foundation of wood carving. I devised those projects to demonstrate the basic concepts and techniques of carving with hand tools and to help you develop the skills they require. Power carving simply takes these fundamentals and speeds them up.

Although the tools may seem very different, and their speed and ease of use can appear almost dauntingly accelerated, power tools are designed to mimic the same tools and procedures we've been using throughout this book. Once you gain confidence in the basics of wood carving, power carving can provide an option for streamlining certain processes, while also furnishing its own unique tricks.

In this project, instead of using large gouges for roughing out, I'll demonstrate the use of a Foredom flexible-shaft tool fitted with Karbide Kutzall® carving balls. This setup is very spontaneous and efficient; it cuts in all directions...so that you can work over the whole carving with absolutely no concern for what direction the grain is going. I load each size cutter in a separate handpiece, so that I can quickly change them as I work. For the detail work, I use a variable-speed electric hand grinder with a variety of finer-grit burrs.

In this project I also present the technique of woodburning, or pyrography, for incising the fine lines of the fur and for undercutting and outlining areas. With woodburning you can create very realistic-looking fur, hair, and feathers on your carvings.

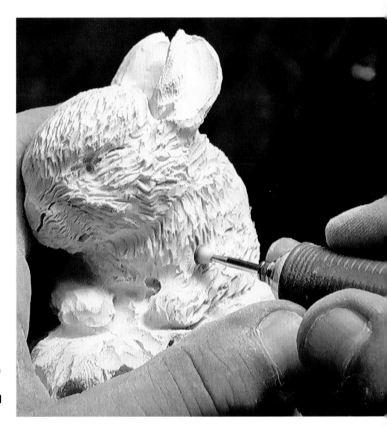

CARVING FINE DETAILS Although you can get some dramatic details with hand tools, power carving makes quick work of creating natural looking fur and feathers on wildlife projects.

Rough out the shape

AS I MENTIONED EARLIER (P. 20), TUPELO is the best wood for power carving. I bandsawed the rough silhouette of the rabbit and lopped off a few corners to get closer to the shape of the design and to reduce the amount of wood to be removed by carving.

1. Bolt the bandsawn block to a work positioner so that you can free both hands and keep them away from the cutters as you work **(PHOTO A)**. Mark a centerline on the wood. Position the pattern on the block and draw the general outlines of the rabbit, centered on the leaf, and some of the leaf scallops to guide you as you carve. Sketch the mound of his haunch where his right foot is raised, scratching his cheek.

2. Put on a dust mask, safety glasses, and earplugs. If you are using a dust collector, position it just behind your workpiece **(PHOTO B)**. If you have more than one handpiece, outfit them with the bits or tips you plan to use. That makes switching cutters faster once you've started the work.

Continued on p. 146.

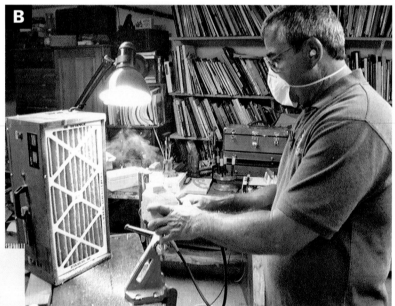

WORK SMART

Try to visualize the rabbit within the wood block, and—as many sculptors have tried to describe it—remove everything that is not the rabbit. This may not work for you the first time, but a little practice will develop the connection between your brain and your fingers.

Whenever I'm carving something as detailed as a fox, a bobcat, a rabbit, or a cardinal, I surround myself with as much reference material as I can. Minor details make a difference. Familiarizing yourself with your subject and studying its anatomy are essential to a successful carving, so that the fox you carve looks like a fox and not a donkey.

I've built up a lifelong collection of reference books. I tear photos out of magazines and file them, so when I'm carving a wolf, I can pull the "Wolves & Coyotes" file and pick photos of various angles of faces, fur textures, and attitudes of the animal. We all know what a cat looks like. But if most of us were asked to draw a picture of a cat, it probably wouldn't look very much like one unless we had the cat, or a picture of it, in front of us for reference.

I also have a collection of actual findings from nature—almost anything I'd want to use in a wildlife or natural still-life carving. I have quite a cache of dried, curled leaves of all varieties. Acorns, moss, milkweed pods, rose hips—they can add a sense of realism and vitality to a composition, but they're hard to carve if you don't really understand their structure, size, and proportion. I even save interesting insects and animal skeletons. The more familiar you become with your subject, the more authentic and natural you'll be able to make your work.

Continued from p. 144.

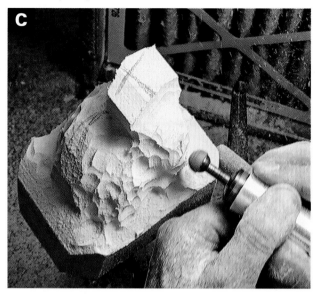

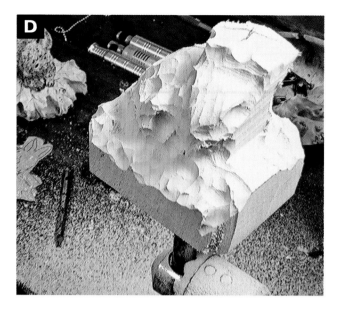

over the whole piece until you have the basic shape pretty well defined **(PHOTO C)**.

4. Fairly quickly, you should have the head shape outlined, along with the areas where the rabbit's eyes and nose will be **(PHOTO D)**. The little lump of his right haunch should be distinct, working up into the shoulders and the raised foot. Fashion the back side so you can get the hind leg on his left.

5. Now take the smaller, ³⁄₁₆-in. ball cutter. It's fairly similar to a 9/6 gouge and can get into some of the more intricate areas. Work a little more on the face, getting the paws down, generally refining more of the finer aspects of the shapes **(PHOTO E)**.

3. Start with your flexible-shaft tool fitted with a ½-in. Kutzall coarse carbide carving ball or equivalent. This large cutter does the same work as the big rough-out gouges, only faster. Start removing wood to rough out the general shape of the rabbit. Begin forming the top of the base, leveling and rounding it over. Continue working

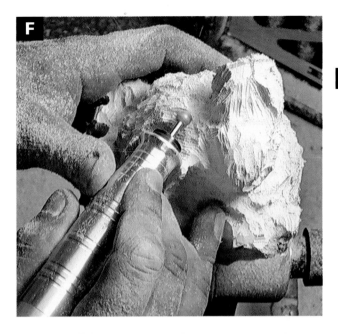

LEAF PATTERNS

The best way to carve leaves or flowers is to have one sitting next to you, so you can see the curves and intricacies firsthand. I used a nicely curled maple leaf as a model for this project. Since the rabbit is sitting on it, you won't see the whole leaf, so I just ripped off the tips and arranged them on the base, sticking the tips out from beneath the animal in a way that pleased me.

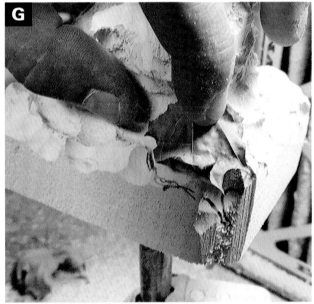

6. Continue using the ³⁄₁₆-in. ball cutter as you would the 9/6 gouge, creating the eyes, the eye troughs, and the top of the head and ears. Do some of the undercutting around the lower jaw area and form the back haunch and the raised hind foot (**PHOTO F**).

7. Leaf tips curling upward in a carving would be fragile and susceptible to breakage, so curl them down into your carving. Trace them onto the base so that you can shape them precisely (**PHOTO G**).

8. Start in again with the small cutter, and recess the background around the contours of the leaf tips (**PHOTO H**). Shape and round the downward curves of the leaves.

Refine the details

NOW THAT WE'VE ROUGHED THE RABBIT out, we'll switch to finer cutters for the detail work. Compare the photos below. **PHOTO A** represents approximately what the project should look like at this stage. **PHOTO B** is a similar—but finished— rabbit that will give you some idea of where your carving should be headed.

To get there, start the details with a bullet-nosed, or flame-shaped, Kutzall burr or equivalent. The teeth are smaller than those on the cutters previously used. For the finer work we'll do now, a micro-motor hand grinder is preferable to the flexible-shaft tool, since the former is better balanced and generates virtually no vibration. I leave the workpiece on the work positioner shaft, but use my hands to steady it while I do this more intricate carving (just as I do when working with fine gouges and knives). *Continued on p. 150.*

A

B

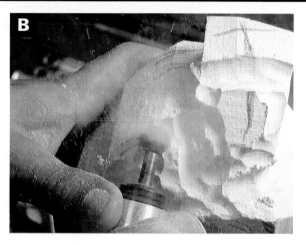

Just as with hand-tool use, there are many grips for holding and working with power carving tools.

There's the pencil grip **(PHOTO A)**, the fist grip—as you'd hold a hammer—**(PHOTO B)**, the flashlight grip **(PHOTO C)**, even the steak-knife

grip, and any and all variations. They should all be firmly braced and guided by thumbs, back fingers, and/or the entire left hand, as you see in the photos.

Since power carving happens quickly, accidents can also be lightning-fast. When the grinder is cutting, it can have a tendency to catch and spin away out of control if it's not firmly anchored. As with knives and gouges, the closer you are to the cutting edge, the more safety and control you have. I try to get right up on it.

Some handpieces have a safety flange on the end **(PHOTO D)**, as opposed to a simple, straight shaft, as seen in **PHOTO E**. The flange is designed to prevent your fingers from sliding forward, into harm's way.

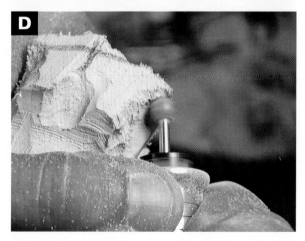

Continued from p. 148.

1. Use the tapered carbide cutter to further delineate the detail and the rabbit's anatomical structures **(PHOTO A)**. Define the contours of the head and face, the eyes and eye channels, the nose, cheeks, back, rump, tail, haunches, paws, and upturned foot—all the elements of the rabbit. Refine the ears and ear cavities, and the body shape.

2. Now we also can shape the leaves a little more, and undercut them further **(PHOTO B)**. With power tools, undercutting is no problem. You can go as deep and as far as the bit will allow, and just sink it right in, easily and cleanly. With gouges, undercutting takes a little more time and finesse.

3. Carve the curls and outline the points of the leaves **(PHOTO C)**.

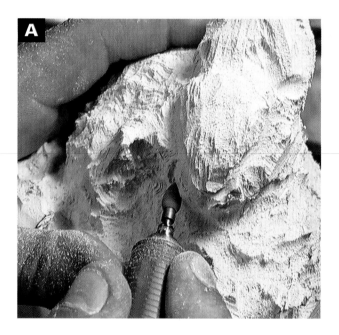

4. At this point, we're going to use some finer-grit stone burrs **(PHOTO D)**. First I use a narrow, pointed, diamond detail bit (top in photo). This little tool takes the place of a detail knife.

5. Work on the fine aspects of the carving: Delineate the nose, muzzle, and the split in the mouth **(PHOTO E)**. Get up in between the ears, separating and shaping them. Accent the fur pushed up where the ears meet the head and some of the final forms of the rabbit.

6. You can dig right in rather deeply in swooping curves to outline the leaves and define the main veins **(PHOTO F)**.

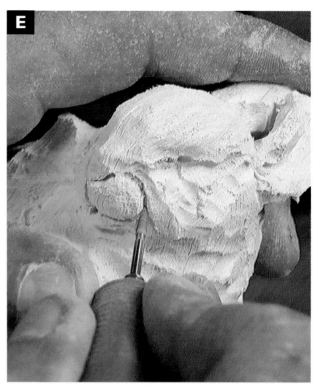

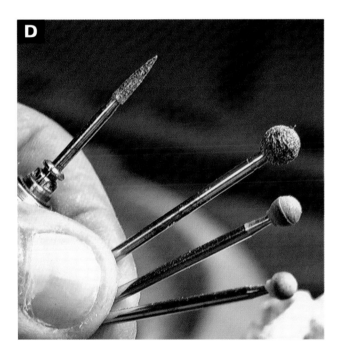

7. I went back, here, and grabbed the ³/₁₆-in. carbide ball cutter and the Foredom tool again to create a grassy overhang with a somewhat ragged, undercut dirt bank around the back of the carving (**PHOTO G**). Then I quickly deepened the background behind the leaves to give a little more dimension to the front.

There are ways to simulate a variety of textures with power tools. We'll create fur texture, the ripples and bug holes of craggy leaves, and the little particles of sandy dirt.

POWER CARVING STONES

The fine-grit colored power carving stones are composed of relatively soft particles. When they get clogged, clean them by running your hand grinder at a slow speed and rolling the burr against a dressing stone.

The photo at right demonstrates this process (with the burr out of its handpiece). The cleaning makes the power carving stone somewhat smaller, so eventually you have to replace it. You can purposely diminish its size if you need a smaller ball, and you also can reshape a burr to suit your purpose.

This photo shows a conical white stone I use to create fur textures. I put a sharp edge on it before each use.

The red ruby and diamond stones are permanently shaped, and cannot be sharpened or dressed. Once they get dull and worn out, you have to replace them. Occasionally they can get clogged. To clean them, I soak them for an hour or so in a film canister with oven cleaner in it to dissolve the compacted wood particles.

Create textures

THE NEXT STONE IS CALLED A RED RUBY.
It's shown second from the top in the **PHOTO D**
on p. 151, and its cutting particles are a little more
aggressive than the diamond detail bit. Use the red
ruby ball in the hand grinder to set up the general
flow of the fur, which you'll define in more detail
later. The pattern of fur runs in flowing curves along
the body at a roughly 45° angle on either side of the
spine, from the back of the head toward the tail.

1. Follow the contours of the shape of the rabbit
with curving lines along the haunches and thighs,
swirling the fur downward toward his bottom
(PHOTO A). You can draw in pencil lines and follow
them, curving up from the eyes toward the center of
the head and running back, meeting at the back of
the head and flowing between the ears.

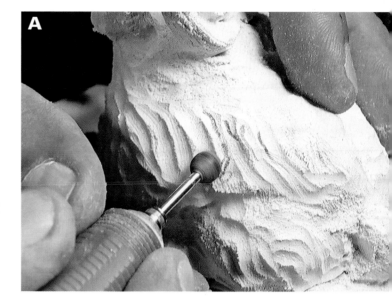

2. The lines on the head and face are subtler
(PHOTO B). Every once in a while, change the flow
from the established direction and undercut the fur.
Smooth the contours of the leaves and the shape of
the mossy embankment.

3. Use a flame-tip diamond bit to smooth over
the ears, thin their edges, and make them more
delicate. Wiggle the bit along to create a casual
separation between the rabbit's body and the
leaves **(PHOTO C)**.

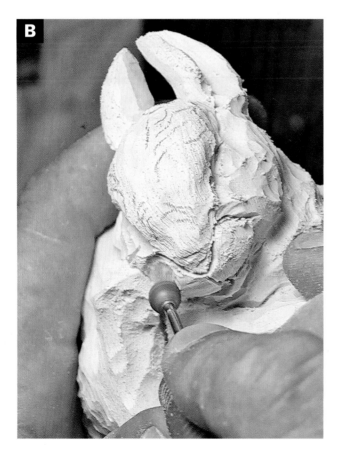

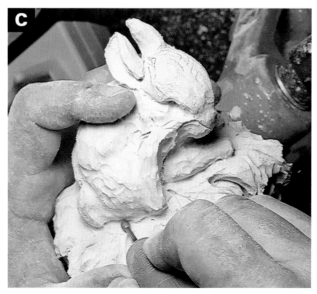

4. Use the conically-shaped white stone as you would a 16/3 V-tool. Make short, curving lines to create the texture of the fur, following the contours you put in with the ball **(PHOTO D)**. Run the motor at a medium speed. Use your thumb as a pivot point, much in the same way you would handle carving tools. With a pencil grip on the handpiece,

bounce and sway to make lazy S-shapes. When you hold the carving in your hand, you can turn the tool and the piece in unison, sweeping the stone in and around to follow the contours of the rabbit. This is a fast and lively swirling technique.

5. The fur on the face is shorter than the longer and more fluid cuts for the rest of the body **(PHOTO E)**. The flow of the fur converges between the ears like water between two rocks, then flairs out again.

WORK SMART

Since microgrinders have a snap chuck, you can't tighten it down and the bit may slip. When you notice the visible length of the shaft increasing, stop and reposition it.

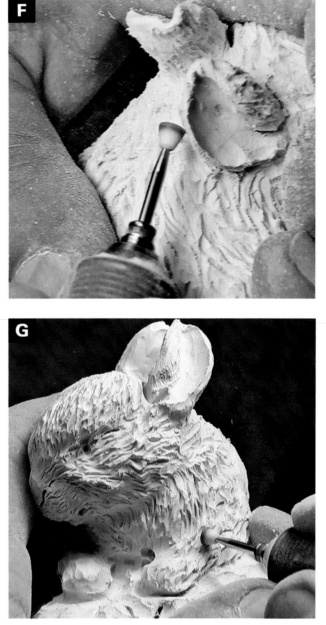

6. Continue around the whole body, ears, and the tail **(PHOTO F)**.

7. Periodically, make a deeper cut to get some shadows in the fur and to bust up the pattern so that it looks more natural **(PHOTO G)**.

8. Now switch to a round blue stone (shown third from the top in **PHOTO D** on p. 151). This is a finer stone than the diamond and is good for smoothing

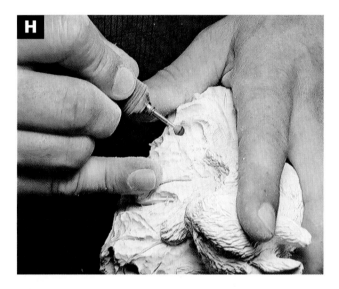

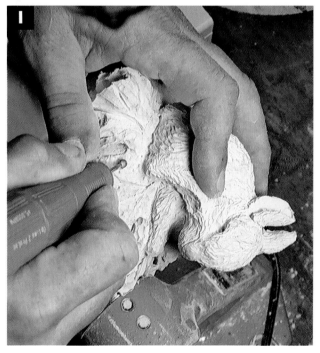

surfaces previously cut with rougher burrs. Make the smooth-surfaced lumps and bumps on the curled leaf. This stone shapes and burnishes in one step, whereas if you were using hand tools, you'd have to come back and smooth down the cuts with sandpaper.

Use your thumb as a pivot and move the stone in a figure-eight motion, going down or up as you create the gnarled texture **(PHOTO H)**. Soften up the heavy depressions of the main veins put in earlier. On the top of a leaf, the veins are generally raised ridges, while on the underside they are hollow. You can show their undersides or their top surface, but once you make a decision, stick to it—don't mix them up on the same leaf surface. You also can come underneath, and smooth the background and the other sides of the leaves. Also texture the dirt under the overhang at the back of the base.

9. Use a smaller bit at this point, a white stone (shown at bottom of **PHOTO D** on p. 151)—which is the finest grit yet—ground to a smaller diameter on a dressing stone. This bit will produce the finer lumps and bumps on the leaves **(PHOTO I)**. You also can put in the smaller secondary veins, and can work on the layers of dirt.

WORK SMART

Hand grinders have variable-speed motors. Set the speed according to the rate at which you move the tool over the wood. You can run the motor at a good clip if you're moving and bouncing along quickly. If you are carving slowly, reduce the grinder speed to avoid burning the wood.

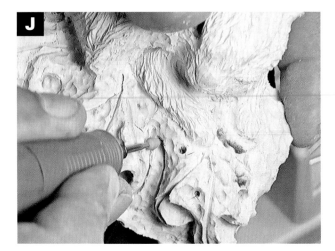

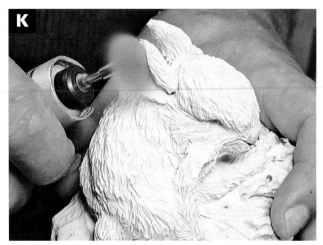

10. The final bit is another fine white stone. This one has a pointed, tapered cone shape that's good for creating the particles of a sandy dirtlike texture beneath the leaves and the grassy overhang. Haphazardly stipple with the tip, poking and rolling it. Then pop a couple of random bug holes into the leaves by poking the tip in here and there at different depths, using a fairly slow motor speed **(PHOTO J)**.

11. There are probably some fuzzies still hanging on the surface, which you can clean up by cutting out a small disk from a green Scotch-Brite pad and mounting the disk on a mandrel for the flexible-shaft tool. Go over the whole carving at the highest possible speed, and the fibers will smooth any rough or hanging bits without damaging the intricately carved texture **(PHOTO K)**.

Woodburning

IF YOU LIKE THE COARSE FUR TEXTURE THE way that stoning leaves it, you can start painting and skip this next section. However, woodburning can add refinement and a dynamic realism to a carving. In addition to the fine fur texture, woodburning can create shadows that will show through the thin washes of oil stains.

1. Roll and twist the knife tip of the woodburner as you would cut the fur texture with a power stone. Make lazy S-shapes, curving off to the right, then toward the left, following the contours of the rabbit and working with the natural flow of the fur you created earlier **(PHOTO A)**.

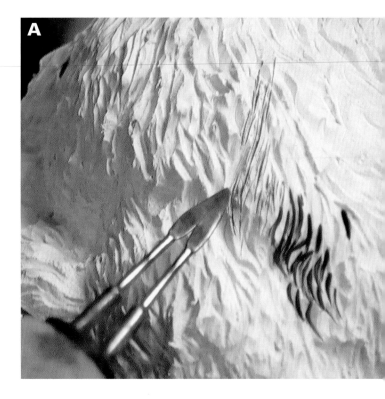

2. Every once in a while, make a deeper cut: let the tip sit on the wood and go just a little further. Wiggle the tip back and forth to create a split in the fur (**PHOTO B**).

3. The woodburner also is used to accent transition points. At the transition between the fur of the arm and the top of the leaves, make a few little curls of fur that just splay onto the surface of the leaves in a natural, unkempt way as though pressed there by the rabbit's weight (**PHOTO C**). Where the leaves and the ground come together is an excellent place for a shadow. Go ahead and turn the temperature up a little, to create a nice deep accent.

4. You can make some bug holes with the woodburner tip as well: sink, twist and wiggle it a bit to create a round hole (**PHOTO D**).

5. The hair inside a young rabbit's ears is extremely fine, and carving would create a heavy texture. Turn the temperature down a bit and woodburn light little marks to simulate that gossamer hair. It has a flow, emanating out of the ear canal. Follow the contour with some wiggles and curls. Working fairly quickly will leave a finer line than moving slowly **(PHOTO E)**.

7. You can carve the bunny's eyes or you can use glass eyes. With realistic wildlife work, I think the glass eyes really kick it up a notch. I used 6-mm, #4 medium brown eyes for the rabbit. Hold the eye up to the carving to get an idea of proper placement **(PHOTO G)**. Look at the head from the top to make sure the eyes are placed symmetrically. Drill a hole, mix up two-part ribbon epoxy, fill the hole with the epoxy, squeeze the eyes in, and create the eyelid.

6. Now, for the cheeks and muzzle—again, fine hairs—use quick, short, light lines. I usually attach paintbrush bristles for whiskers, but you can make a quick little spin with the tip of the wood-burner to make the little follicles that hold the whiskers **(PHOTO F)**.

8. The eyelids on the right eye are different from the other, because his foot is pushing his cheek up so that his eye isn't completely open. You can create this effect with the epoxy **(PHOTO H)**. Refer to the duck decoy for a more detailed description of creating eyelids. You can play with it a little; if

Each woodburning tip will burn differently at the same setting, and each type of wood you use will burn differently also—depending on its density, grain pattern, and moisture content.

Take a scrap piece and make a few test marks before you work on your carving. With a knife tip, you should be able to essentially draw with the tool.

At a proper lower setting, your tip should sink into the wood just enough to make a crisp, smooth line as shown at center in the photo at right. At too high a setting, the wood burns so fast that the tool plunges into the wood, and the burn mark becomes wider and sloppy (left line in the photo). You don't have as much control when you're burning at that high a setting, and it throws up smoke and blackens the wood. If the setting is even higher, you risk setting your piece on fire (at right in the photo). You're looking for a medium toast kind of color, not too black, but also not so inconspicuous you won't notice it.

The other factor is the speed at which you move the tool. Every time the tip touches the wood it cools down somewhat, and then it has to heat up again to its given temperature setting. If you are a slower,

more methodical woodburner, you may want to use a lower temperature, because you're sitting on that line slightly longer than if you were going fast, and it's going to heat up.

Rule of thumb: Burn lightly first. It's easy to go back to accent and darken some areas, but once you char that surface, the mark is not going away.

you don't like it, pull the eye out, mix up some new epoxy, and try it again.

9. Another important use I have for a woodburner is to create my signature (**PHOTO** I). Every carving I've ever done since I was a child has always been signed and dated. Some people use a stamp, some an engraver or power carving burr, and some simply a felt pen. Because I put so much time and so much of myself into a carving, I think taking the time to put a personal signature on it is a really nice touch. I've developed a special signature to burn onto my carvings. If you like this technique, practice and work up one of your own. Refer to "Power-carved rabbit" on p. 181 for instructions on painting this figure.

Bark Carvings

AS YOU BECOME COM-fortable with basic wood carving skills and techniques, you may become curious and find yourself looking for other, more unusual, directions for your craft—experimenting with bought or found materials, for example. There is an unlimited supply of uncommon stuff to carve, from tagua nuts (so-called vegetable ivory), bone, or antler, to assorted vacation discoveries like coconut shells, or tree branches you can carve into walking sticks.

The distinctive feature about bark is its rugged, wild cragginess. The bark surface also becomes a natural frame around your carving. Because of these qualities, bark lends itself to nature and wildlife carvings, like the bird you see in the center of the photo at right, or bears and the like.

You can use some of the material's innate characteristics in your carving. Common subjects include fantasy castles and cottages—oddly shaped little homes with windows and Escher-like staircases rolling up and down.

ONE MATERIAL I'M FOND OF IS THE THICK bark from the cottonwood tree. Cottonwood bark grows in chunky formations around the trunk. Almost triangular in cross-section and resembling cogs on a gear, the bark is harvested by splitting it off in variously sized blocks. It's softer than regular lumber, so it's easier and quicker to carve, and it has a wonderful, swirly grain. The bark's crevices and crannies can transform into rooftops, splits between buildings, natural shadows, and so on. However, the texture is rather crumbly, so it doesn't take fine details.

This earthy material can yield a striking sculpture if you work within its parameters. In this project we're going to carve the face of an old Indian man. There's an obvious reason why a Native American elder would be a comfortable and dignified subject for a piece of cottonwood bark. A clown, on the other hand, would not be as suitable a choice. Choose a design that works with the nature and shape of the material. In this case, the texture of the bark can also lend a weathered look to the face of this figure, or any figure of some age.

Work gingerly and gently when shaping details, making stop cuts, and putting in shadows. Since bark is flaky and tends to crumble and tear more than other woods, it's critical to have a very sharp edge on your hand tools so they slice easily through with very little pressure on the fibers.

You also can power carve this material. The blue-bird with the flower shown in the center of the photo on the facing page was all power carved. Once again, work carefully without exerting a lot of force against the piece. Woodburning also accentuates details nicely and creates shadows and depth on bark carvings.

I think a natural finish is the best way to go for most work done on cottonwood bark. That treatment brings out the shadows and undercuts, and retains the natural character of the material. If you like, you can highlight shadows with an oil stain that's slightly darker than the natural finish you apply.

MAKING BRIDGES Bark is not very strong, so when you carve out sections like the window openings on a cottage, leave connective bridges joining the hollows all the way through to the back of the piece.

Rough in the design

DON'T WORRY TOO MUCH IF THERE'S A small crack in your bark. As long as it has enough integrity to hold together (as long as the wood doesn't split), cracks and other imperfections just add to the rustic feel. As with most small projects,

this one is best done handheld, with the care and tool control discussed in previous chapters.

1. First, scrape off the shaggy surface bark and smooth a fairly level area big enough for the face. The big blade of a jackknife is great for this and will quickly hog out a clear space (**PHOTO A**).

2. Decide where the image would look best on your workpiece (slightly off center in one direction

CAPTURING THE ESSENCE

When you are doing a carving, you are obviously trying to get the technique, placement, and proportion right. Equally important is capturing the essence of the subject.

Carving isn't just about reproduction. A skilled craftsperson strives to bring out the meaning and feeling of what he or she is carving—what makes that animal or that person tick, what

they are all about. An image of a mother rabbit and her baby can express tenderness; you can show strength and power in a grizzly bear or a lion.

In this venerable face, we're not looking for an expressionless cigar-store Indian. Depth and shadows, and the structure of facial forms (cheekbones, eye sockets, angle of the nostrils, lips, a strong chin) can convey

a sense of power and dignity, pride and respect.

The eyes are very expressive. They're the first thing anyone looks at in a carving, just as you first look for the eyes of each living person you meet. You want to give this Native American wise, expressive eyes. Create a sense of depth, strength, and wisdom with undercuts, shaping, and deep shadows.

or another generally is most pleasing). In this case, a little below center seems best, to make room for the feather sticking up. Because this rough surface makes a carbon-paper transfer difficult, use dividers to transfer the parameters of the face from the drawing to the wood. Make reference marks for distances (the bottom of the nose to the chin, etc.), outline the face, and sketch in the features **(PHOTO B)**.

3. With a 15/6 V-tool, delineate the eyes, nose, and mouth, as well as the other details **(PHOTO C)**.

4. A small veining gouge or a round-bottomed 14/10 V-tool will help you refine the facial features **(PHOTO D)**. As you get deeper into the cottonwood, it becomes more structurally sound.

5. Take a small veiner, say an 11/4 tool, and outline the head. Accentuate the prominent cheekbones by carving hollows underneath **(PHOTO E)**.

6. Refine the eyes, nose, mouth, chin, and the curving lines around the mouth from nose to chin that define the bottom of the cheeks **(PHOTO F)**.

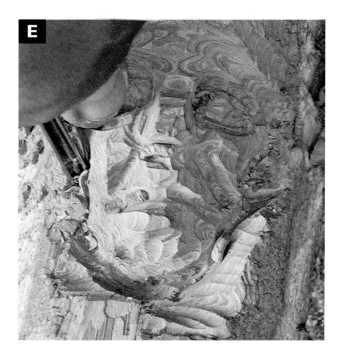

7. Take a look at the side view of the piece and see how the profile looks, then adjust anything that needs it **(PHOTO G)**. Look down from the top to see if the eyes are even and at an equal depth. Check the roundness of the cheeks and the position of nostrils to make sure the whole face is evolving symmetrically.

Even as you're maneuvering the work, always keep a good grip on the tool. Keep your hands very close to the cutting edge, and use your other fingers as guides, supports, and pivot points.

Refine the details

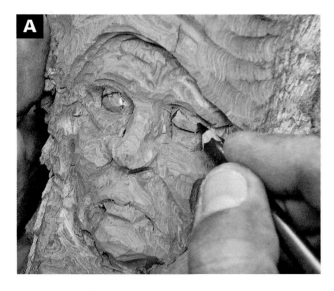

2. Make semicircular stop cuts with tight slits below to create the V-cuts that outline the eyelids with distinct shadows. Round the eyes, from the tear duct at the inside corner to the outside corner **(PHOTO B)**.

1. Sketch in the eyes, bringing the eyelids slightly downward so they're somewhat thoughtful and heavy, to reflect age and wisdom **(PHOTO A)**. Use a detail knife to refine and clean up the forms. Shape simple lumps of wood to simulate eyebrows.

3. Make a nice undercut to create the deep shadow of a very slight opening between the lips **(PHOTO C)**. When carving a mouth, this is always an effective treatment. It creates the sense of breathing and life that a face with tightly closed lips can't convey. Put in the nostrils with the same techniques used in the knife-carved Santa (see pp. 41–43).

4. This is an old outdoorsman, so he's going to have some wrinkles and weathering. Use the small V-tool to create some lines underneath the bags of his eyes and some deep creases between the brows. Wiggle a few age wrinkles in on the upper lip and on the cheekbones **(PHOTO D)**. Delineate the outside

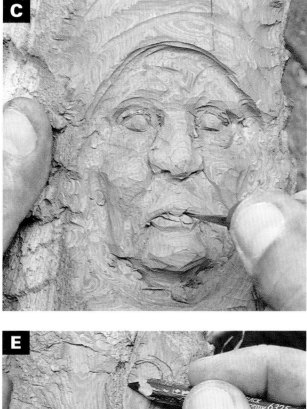

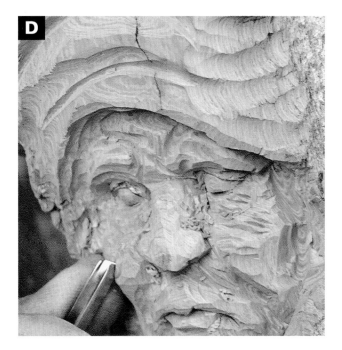

perimeter of his face with the V-tool, to give a little more shadow. But don't lose that nice natural bark edge around the carving. Outline a headband with the V-tool. Use a bigger veiner to shape the curved roll of the headband. Use your imagination for any other details you may want to add—a bear claw necklace or whatever.

5. Sketch in a gently curving feather above the head. I drew a big eagle feather with a little split in

it and tried to use my bark's natural crack as a visual element in the feather **(PHOTO E)**. Back-cut around the outline to recess the background. A veiner can give some contour to the feather's surface. Use a V-tool to carve the main vein, and then create the lines of the feather detail, and put in some hair. A part in the middle might look good, or the hair might look better pulled back, maybe with a braid coming down.

6. Give some detail to the eyebrows (**PHOTO F**).

7. Use dividers to mark the spot for a little hole in each eye that will give direction to his gaze (**PHOTO G**). The hole collects stain and that creates a shadow as a reverse highlight (if you were painting the eyes you'd put a little white dot on each one). Place each hole off center, so he appears to be looking up or down, right or left—anywhere but dead straight ahead, as that'll drain the life out of his expression. Use the tip of an awl to make the hole.

8. You also can use the tip to stipple in a beadwork design on the headband (**PHOTO H**). You don't want to go very deep, as the wood is fragile. Light, shallow dots will create enough shadow to stand out, especially once they fill with stain. Use a small gouge to carve the little trough on the upper lip.

9. The back side of the bark has a lot of rather shaggy-looking stringy fibers. You can use a belt sander to flatten the whole back so it sits flat against the wall, but I like to remove the ragged surface and level the back with a large, fairly flat gouge (**PHOTO I**). Sign the back of your carving if you like, and drill a little hole in the back so you can hang it up on a nail. Don't let the drill pull itself completely through the front of your carving.

10. We're finished. Now brush on one coat of Minwax Natural finish (**PHOTO J**). Just cover the carved part; if you apply the stain to the rough bark surface, it darkens too much and kills the rustic light-gray patina. The shadows in the carving deepen and darken with the stain. If you want, you can highlight certain areas with a darker stain, or even use oil paints to accent the face or beadwork. The Minwax stain is all the finish needed, though if you want to seal the entire surface without changing the color, you can spray it with semigloss acrylic after the stain has dried for a couple of days.

F

G

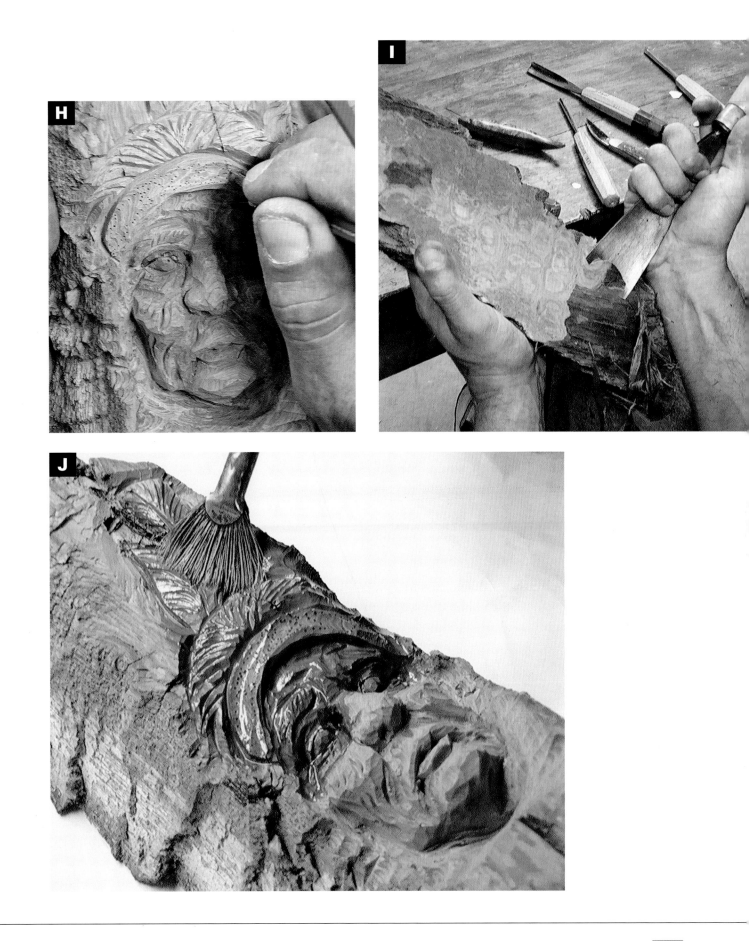

Painting and Finishing

SO YOU'VE SPENT A lot of time carefully carving your project, and you'd like to add some color. First of all, after expending all that skill and effort, don't try to compress the painting step into a rushed ten-minute session. Give yourself ample time to sit down, relax, and enjoy the process of making your carving spring to life. It's really not difficult.

First think of a color scheme, and consider how the colors are going to interact to complement the carving. In this chapter, I'll discuss some cool effects, like tonal changes, highlights, shadows, and echoing color.

Be open to new ideas that may come as you work, but do stop at that elusive "good enough" point. Your finish should integrate itself into the overall formation of the carving. The color schemes, blending, shading, and highlighting will all have an important effect on the final appearance of a piece. You don't want the paint to overpower or detract from your work. Rather, let it be the whipped cream on top.

SOMETIMES, ESPECIALLY WITH WILDLIFE carvings, simply putting a clear (or "natural") finish on the wood is enough. The same holds true for many bark carvings, which seem to spring right from the wood. Minwax Natural is a clear stain, available everywhere paints and stains are sold. It is my finish of choice. I mix it with oil paints, as well as with other oil-based stains and finishes.

Artist's paints come in oils and acrylics. I generally prefer oils for most work, but there are many other wood-carvers who think differently. Each type of paint has its own advantages and its own particular foibles. Oil paints are made for blending, and they do it beautifully and easily. Acrylics don't give you the same workability, but their quick-drying nature enables on-the-spot overpainting and touch ups without delay.

For almost 37 years I've applied paint using a staining technique that has a lot of similarities to watercolor—washes, building up and blending color, and letting it run. I want the grain of the wood to show through. I like each piece to look like a wood carving and not a casting. By thinning the paint down with water (for acrylics) or Minwax Natural (for oil paints), I get the consistency I want. When applied in a thin wash to raw wood, the small amount of paint mixed with the vehicle gets absorbed into the wood pores, creating a depth of color, rather than the superficial application you get when painting on a sealed surface (such as the gessoed decoy).

To complete my painting setup, I place my detail knife close at hand, and maybe a gouge, so that I can clean up any ratty spots I may have overlooked. I also have a cup of water or clear finish for thinning and mixing nearby, and some folded paper towels to catch overflow and for dabbing off the brushes. After trial and error, I've learned that the teacup with paint stain always goes on the left, coffee on the right. You don't want to mix them up.

There's no big mystery to painting. It doesn't have to be a meticulous process; it should be fun. So just spread out, dive in, and slap a little color around. If you make a goof or change your mind, your work can always be touched up later.

FINISHING TOUCHES Painting and finishing means more than simply adding color to a carving. A successful finish will appear to be an integral part of your design and will bring your figures to life.

Using colored pencils

MANY PEOPLE THINK THEY CAN'T PAINT, or they don't want to deal with the process or the mess. Using colored pencils, however, is an option anyone can employ to apply color and bring a carving to life, without paints or brushes.

There are many good-quality, soft-lead colored pencil sets on the market (don't get hard-lead pencils, they score the wood and don't lay down much color). Art supply stores often stock individual pencils that you can try out to see if you like them before you buy a set. My pack is an assortment of 36 made by Lyra®.

A good project that illustrates the ease and versatility colored pencils offer is the carved box lid.

ACCESSING COLORED PENCILS Many tightly packed boxes of colored pencils are ingeniously designed so that you can raise a pencil out by pressing down on its bottom end.

Carved box lid

We'll color the frog design on the round box lid we carved in an earlier chapter (see "Basic outlining," on p. 104). If you have any remaining pencil lines from your pattern transfer, you can remove them now, or leave them to add some extra shadow and dimension. The look is entirely up to you. As you progress, you can quit any time you are satisfied.

1. Start by putting a natural finish on the lid. For some reason, colored pencils go on better when the wood is lightly sealed with Minwax Natural. You can brush it, swab it on with a paper towel, or if the piece is small enough, just dip it right into the can. One coat is enough **(PHOTO A)**.

2. This is a South American male gliding frog about six months old and you can use a photo,

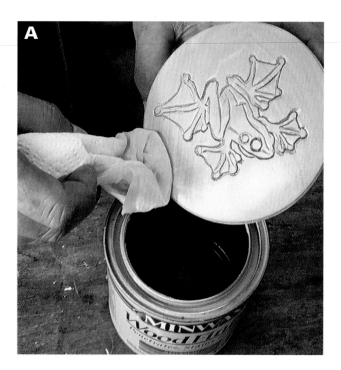

A

WORK SMART

It's easier to blend pencil colors when they are not applied too heavily, so lay your color down lightly at first. To get more color density in a specific area, press harder.

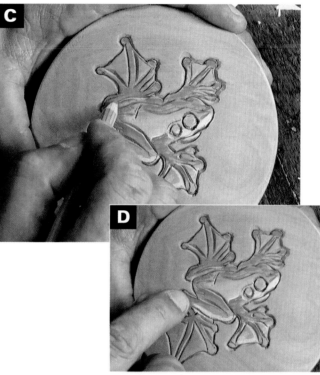

drawing, or painting to select the colors you'll need. I pulled out white, yellow, orange, a medium brown, and black, and some green for the grassy background. Start with the lightest tones first—a little white in the throat area, behind the eardrum, and on the lower leg. Press harder along the lower body, and lighten your touch to fade the color away as you move up higher **(PHOTO B)**. Then start working in some yellow. He has a very yellow eye and some yellow that blends from his orangey back into the white belly area. Rubbing lightly, color in the webbing of the front and rear gliding feet.

3. This is a predominately orange frog, so color the orange areas in, again lightly **(PHOTO C)**.

4. You can rub the pencil marks to soften them, and also blend the transition from orange to yellow to white on the body **(PHOTO D)**. Press harder to accent darker areas of color, to help define the body parts.

5. Since orange is close to brown, use it as an accent color and put in some shadows with a medium brown. Then take out a pure black (I used mars black). Draw the pupil of the frog's eye as kind of a slit. Gently put some darker shadows in and around the webbing areas to add depth and dimension, and blend the colors with your finger **(PHOTO E)**.

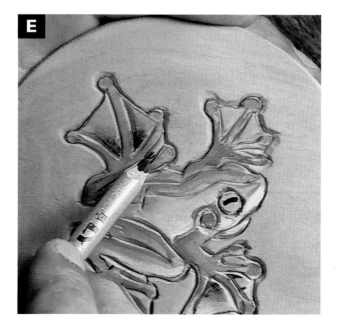

6. Wiggle in little black bands on the body and sketch triangular shapes on the forearm, starting at the back, but don't go all the way around to the front. Then pepper in a few black dots. To produce a more realistic effect, highlight strategically with white to simulate light bouncing off the frog's skin. Make a background. Here, apple green suggests a grassy effect, which gets a little heavier around the legs and feet to create shadow (**PHOTO F**).

7. Fade the color into the natural wood on the rest of the box, smudging it with your finger (**PHOTO G**). Spray the surface with a clear semigloss finish like Deft®, to set the color and keep it from smearing. Some spray finishes will change the pencil colors, so try the acrylic or varnish on a sample scrap first, to see if you like the effect. Oil-soaked rags can be a safety hazard, so dispose of them properly (see "Disposing of rags: Caution!," p. 179).

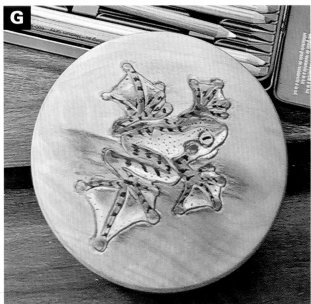

Painting with acrylics

ACRYLICS ARE EASY TO USE, DRY QUICKLY, and require no smelly solvents or flammables—and cleanup is a snap. Acrylic paint dissolves in water for mixing, diluting, and cleanup, but dries to a permanent, waterproof flexible film.

The two most common brands, Golden® and Liquitex®, are high-quality products, available at almost all art supply, hobby, and craft stores. Acrylics can become plastic looking if laid down thickly so I recommend thinning the paint to keep the effect subtle and soft. When you're touching up, remember that acrylics dry a couple shades darker than they look when wet.

Sign painting

Painting letters is somewhat exacting work. Make sure your paint flows easily but not so loosely that it bleeds over the top edges of the letters. A few practice strokes on another board are a good idea.

1. Squeeze out a dab of buff or cream color for the background. Then dip your brush (a round brush large enough to get between the letters with almost one stroke) into the cup of water, and mix the wet brush into a small amount of paint to make a thin wash **(PHOTO A)**.

2. Cut around the letters with this color and try not to let paint run down into the characters

(PHOTO B). If the paint does run down, you can remove it with a knife or paint over it later with the letter color. Blend away the excess in any painted areas you might have painted too heavily.

3. Darken the edge of the background with a little brown tone to give it an aged look. Mix a wash of brown ochre and apply it lightly around the edge. Rub it with your fingers to blend it into the background color you applied in the previous step **(PHOTO C)**.

WORK SMART

Lay a length of wide, plastic-coated freezer wrap across your worktable and use it as a palette, mixing your paints right on the sheet. Tape the edges down.

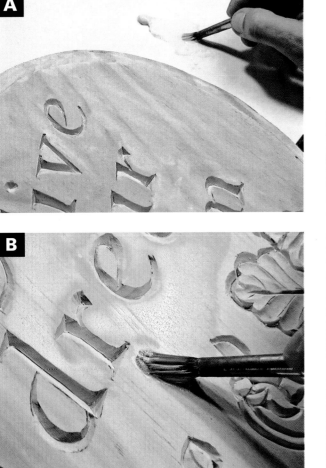

A

B

C

4. Paint the letters with some creamy sap green on a #2 flat brush, being careful not to let the color seep onto the background. However, if you get a little sloppy, go back when the paint is dry and cover it with the background color, mixed a bit thicker than before. When painting the letters, use the flat edge of the brush to pull the paint right up the edge of the cut **(PHOTO D)**.

5. Don't be afraid to modify your colors as you go. For a lighter green, add a little yellow. To give the sign some life and textual interest, keep the mixture uneven so you retain variations in color and tone **(PHOTO E)**.

6. Add a second shade to the letters by striking the left sides of the characters with partial strokes of thin yellow, so that they light up and create a visual depth **(PHOTO F)**. This also will help balance the colors of the final piece, because the flower will have yellow in it, too.

7. Add a little more yellow where the stem enters the bud. For a very soft leaf, really water down the paint. And lighten up the left side of the leaf just a little **(PHOTO G)**. Accentuate the shadows in the junctures within the bud with some darker green and then apply it to the areas where the leaf and the petal meet. Then, for balance, go back and accent the right sides of the letters with the dark green. Use brown for the seed, then highlight it by mixing in some yellow.

8. Paint the front flower and its central nodules yellow with a small amount of napthol red on a flat brush. Let the yellow dry, then stipple the back petals and the darker centers on the front flower with a deep-violet dioxin-purple blend, mixed to a creamy consistency **(PHOTO H)**.

9. Highlight around the violet petal in front with the bristles tipped in white, then shadow some of the purple with an overpaint of napthol red. Then show

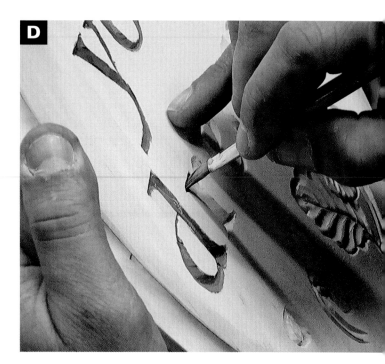

a flower opening out of the bud with a little of the purplish violet—heavier where the bud is coming out of the leaves but lightening out to the tip. Put a dark center on the central flower right between the three stamen-pistil triangles. Outline the grooved border around the plants with brown and detail a little brown vein down the center of the leaf. Since the seed is already brown, outline it with green.

When the sign is dry, go back and touch up any glitches. Add a faint green wash around the coved border.

Once everything has dried for a couple of hours, you could put an oil-based antique finish on it, or leave it just as it is.

WORK SMART

I only use the tip of the brush to apply paint. If you jam the brush into the paint it pushes into the upper bristles and gets stuck there. Then it bleeds into the next color you use.

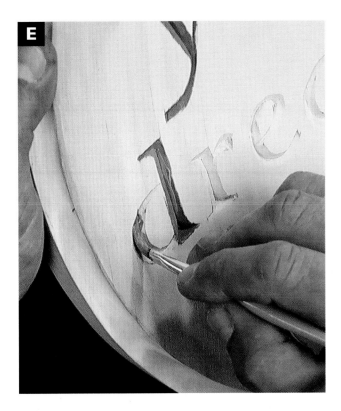

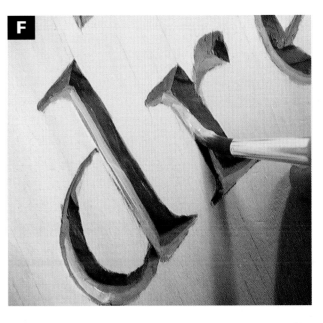

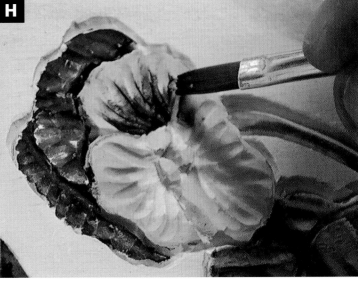

Oil painting

OILS HAVE BEEN THE TRADITIONAL PAINT medium for artists for centuries. The vibrant intensity of oils has a depth and richness unmatched by acrylics, which can have more of a synthetic look.

Oil paints have qualities well suited to thin, stain-like applications on bare wood. Since oils are not thinned with water, they do not raise the grain—creating a fuzzy surface on the wood—as acrylics do. And when the paint is thinned heavily with a self-hardening finish like Minwax Natural, it dries much more quickly than oil paints applied to a gessoed canvas. Being absorbed into and curing in the wood pores also makes the paint become one with the carving.

Old boathouse relief carving

I use Old Holland paints. But there are many quality oil-paint manufacturers. Each company often has different names for its colors.

Minwax Natural is a clear stain we'll use as a vehicle and thinner for the paint, just as water is used with acrylics. To finish the boathouse relief carving, start by squeezing small dabs of the following colors onto the palette, spaced well apart: cobalt blue, sap green, burnt umber, raw umber, mars black, red brown ochre, buff, white, Italian brown pink lake (Old Holland color, similar to burnt sienna), Italian earth (similar to mars yellow), and warm gray (light beige color).

1. Mix a little stain and dab of raw umber into a brushing consistency. Then lighten it with a little brown ochre and thin it to a translucent wash by adding a fair amount of stain. Flow this onto the house siding. A touch of white will lighten some of the middle areas of siding. Wiggle in a darker color, Italian brown pink lake (or burnt sienna) to create shadowing underneath the roof and along the front corner. The shingles along the back side of the house can be darker **(PHOTO A)**.

2. Mimic an old gray undercoat on the house with a little white with a very small mix of cobalt blue, some black and a little raw umber. (Just mix the

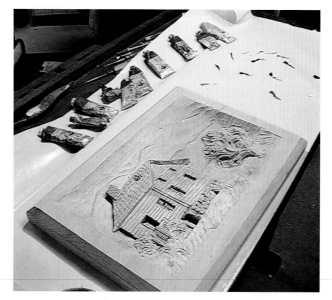

COVER YOUR TABLE SURFACE with the freezer-wrap palette, and lay out your carving, paints, brushes, detail knife, paper towel, and a small cup of Minwax Natural.

paints together quickly, to maintain color variations as you apply the paint.) With a small amount on your brush, bring out this cobalt gray in faint patches on the door, the window frames, and across the center areas of the siding. Then darken the frame around the windows with more brown. For the stone foundation, dab a little Italian earth (or mars yellow) with a little white, raw umber, and buff.

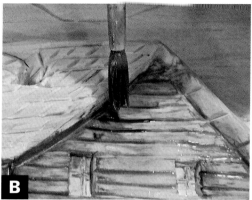

3. Make the shadow color real loose (thin), and just touch the siding here and there. The paint will run along the V-cuts in between the clapboards, making it look as though you painted each line individually. Start uphill, and the paint will flow downward (**PHOTO B**). You can wipe some off the surface, but it will remain as shadows in between the boards. Do this on the front side of the house, too. You can even blow on it to increase the flow.

MIXING COLORS

Mixing colors is one of the exciting aspects of painting. By playing with variations of tones, lights and darks, and highlights and shadows, you'll be amazed at how dynamic your work can become.

There are several kinds of colors. Prismatic colors are those right out of the tube. Tints have white added to them. Darkened gray tones incorporate black. There are loud neon hues, as well. What I use most in my work are earth tones—colors with shades of brown added in. They are subdued tones, more like those you'd find in nature.

THE SPICY VARIETY OF LIFE
When you think of a tree, you know it has green leaves, but when you look closely, you see an endless variation of color as the light hits the leaves from different angles.

When I mix paints for natural subjects, I don't want to turn any color into a single hue. If you're mixing colors, just swirl the brush in them quickly, so each stroke lays down a slightly different shade. That way you capture more vitality in your painting. The brush strokes themselves create movement.

LIGHTEN UP
Many people think the only way to lighten a color is to add white. When you're painting green plants, use yellow to achieve a lighter shade that's more earthy and outdoorsy.

Also use yellow to lighten browns. Some browns are a more reddish, orangey yellow, like burnt sienna and ochre; others are blacker, like burnt umber and raw umber. But all browns contain oranges and yellows. You can even get interesting effects on browns with red and orange, as well as yellow. Black by itself is a dull, flat color, so I usually add ultramarine or cobalt blue to bring it to life. If the carving has a lot of red, I'll add red into the black to give it some vibrancy.

Another way to lighten color is by thinning it. You can also use a thinning technique to create a gradual fade-out. Start by applying a heavier coat of color, then take most of the paint off the brush, wet it (in water or oil, depending on the type of paint you're using), and use the tip to subtly pull the paint to gradually fade out the color.

4. Paint the windows with thinned raw umber, one of the blacker browns. Then tip a small #2 round brush into a little white and wiggle some highlights into the dirty windowpanes. Mix more of the cobalt gray, a little tighter this time, and paint the window frames and doors. Put a darker shade on the right side of the door, inside the house, and along the left edge where it meets the frame. Combine some brown and a little blue into mars black till it's a really rich, deep black. Darken the interior openings of the doors and the hanging windowpane as well as the broken pane. Put a bit of shadow along the foundation and under the eaves. Really slop that shadow color around in the hole in the roof **(PHOTO )**. It needs to look dark and unrepaired.

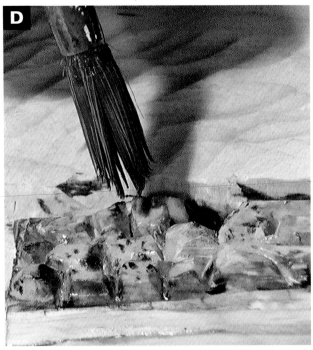

5. Wash the shingled roof in ochre tones, making the shingles a little darker toward the back. Work a small amount of red almost off the brush on the palette, and apply the color to the roof, to differentiate the brown tones on the roof from the siding. To shadow the grooves in the roof, just touch it with a very fine black wash and let the paint run, just like you did on the siding. Create a brick red from Italian brown pink lake and burnt sienna tinged with a small amount of burnt umber and red. Paint the chimney, but don't get any on the background. A touch of white will impart an old, brick-mortar feel. Saturate the hole in the foundation with burnt umber, and while you have it on the brush, throw a little bit around the rocks, letting it flow between them. Then take all the paint off the brush. Dip it lightly into straight black, right from the tube so that the paint just sits on the tips of the brush. Stipple it onto the foundation, to

E

create flecking in the rocks. Then stipple straight white on the foundation to create some glistening crystals (**PHOTO D**).

6. Fill in the pond area with the cobalt gray. Add some raw umber with just a smidgen of white to lighten it up, and paint the rail and stairs with a thin wash. Paint the dark timbers under the central bush with burnt umber. And put a little gray on top of the house to show aged, peeling paint. Subdue

the bright green with a little raw umber and dab this earth-toned wash into the bushes and tree. It should run and pool in the carved shadows, really popping out the depth in the bushes. Make it a little darker on the bottom to show some shadow, as well as in the tree's center, working in some brown tones. Stipple little leaves in varying shades of green onto the tree, as you did when speckling the stones (**PHOTO E**).

DISPOSING OF RAGS: CAUTION!

When using any oil- or solvent-based finish, such as Minwax Natural Stain, it's essential that you dispose of finish-soaked rags or paper towels properly to avoid spontaneous combustion! If left unattended (in a pile on your garage floor, for example), they can generate enough heat to catch fire on their own. We've spoken with several people who have lost their homes or workshops to fire because of oil-soaked rags. These materials should be tossed into a metal bucket of water to soak, then hung out flat to dry, and then be disposed of later. They also can be burned outdoors in a tall metal canister under careful supervision.

Never pour finish wastes down a drain.

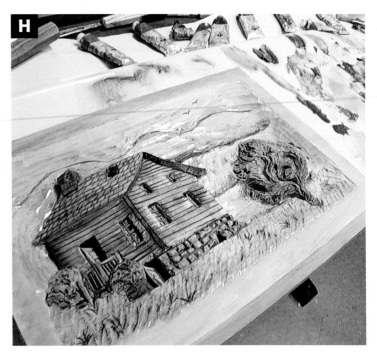

7. Put some shadows in for tree branches, using burnt umber with a small amount of white. This grayish brown will balance the color in the windows. Make the grass a softened, earth-toned green to coincide with early spring. The color seeps nicely into the weeds cut with the V-tool. To avoid a hard edge around the frame, bleed some of the color gently into the frame area. Tap darker greens into the foreground, to bring it closer to you **(PHOTO F)**. Darken the water with raw umber near the shoreline, and add a bit of white to let the water fade into the horizon. Color the field in the background with a very thin green wash, making it a little deeper in the foreground to give a gentle roll to the bank. Every so often, flick a little brush stroke of deeper color here and there to simulate something like sage brush growing too far away to clearly see. Color the faraway mountains with a soft brownish wash, and again have it a little darker on the closer bottom of the hill.

8. Dry touch the chimney with a very thin wash and let it run to subtly accent the brickwork. Color the sky with a light gray wash, like you used on the windowsills, with maybe a little white here and there to simulate clouds. Paint the gulls a darker grayish color. Shadow the railing with straight raw umber on a #1 detail brush. Shadow around the bush and under the chimney a little more, and put a few shadows into the stonework to create more depth **(PHOTO G)**.

9. To help the color of the frame echo the gray shades used elsewhere in the carving, mix white, cobalt blue, a small amount of black, and raw umber. Paint the frame with the grain, keeping the wash fairly light **(PHOTO H)**.

Power-carved rabbit

HERE IS ANOTHER EXAMPLE OF THE BEAUTY and versatility of oil painting. A power carving finished with woodburned details—like the power-carved rabbit discussed in an earlier chapter—can stand alone, but a light, strategic paint job can really bring it to life.

USE A PAINTING STICK For a piece this small, hold it with a metal painting stick that screws into the bottom of the carving.

1. Start off with some midrange colors. Mix up brown ochre with Minwax Natural into a very thin wash, and paint the rabbit's body **(PHOTO A)**. Thin paint won't stick very well to the epoxy around the eyes, so mix it thicker for this area. Mix in a little Italian earth and make the paws and the feet a lighter color.

2. Mix Old Holland gray light into a thin wash and apply it to the white places on the rabbit's fur—around the tail, on the back haunches, inside the ear, the whisker mound, the belly fur, and the chest area. Paint the leading edge of the ears with burnt umber on a smaller brush, and add some shadows around the tail, the eyelid, behind the eyes, under the chin, in the transition area between the whisker mound and his cheek, and behind and under the upturned foot.

3. Mix some lighter white with mars yellow into a very soft cream color—without clear stain for a technique called dry brushing: Just get enough paint on the bristles so that they stay splayed, and drag them lightly across the fur sideways **(PHOTO B)**. This great highlight effect gives a fine, individual-hair-like quality to the fur. Paint pure white highlights on the muzzle, cheek, and down on the throat, and then paint the white diamond shape on top of the head.

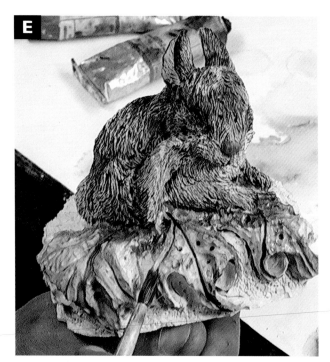

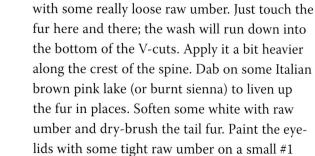

4. Accentuate the shadows in the carved grooves with some really loose raw umber. Just touch the fur here and there; the wash will run down into the bottom of the V-cuts. Apply it a bit heavier along the crest of the spine. Dab on some Italian brown pink lake (or burnt sienna) to liven up the fur in places. Soften some white with raw umber and dry-brush the tail fur. Paint the eyelids with some tight raw umber on a small #1 brush **(PHOTO C)**.

5. Mix an ultramarine blue wash and use it as you used the thin wash of raw umber in step 4. Just a hint of the color in a wash won't turn your carving blue but will create a nice shadow and soften up all the colors. Dab it lightly around **(PHOTO D)**.

6. Paint the leaves green with brown added to warm it up. Then smear a thin wash of raw umber on the leaves here and there **(PHOTO E)**. Create a burnt-umber ultramarine-blue shadow where the

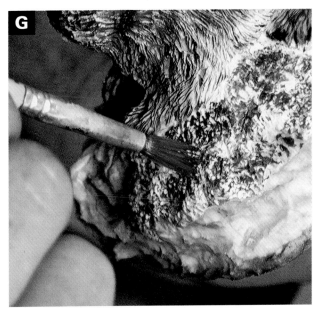

> Instead of using turpentine or other toxic and flammable solvents, I clean my brushes with soap and warm water. It's easy and it keeps the bristles soft and supple.

rabbit is sitting on the leaf. Wiggle the brush to get soft transitions. Touch the leaf tips with a real loose dark brown wash so that it runs into the crevices of the veins.

7. Accentuate the undercuts around and behind the leaves with a fairly tight dark brown shadow. Balance the rabbit's yellow tones with some Italian earth. Outline the bottom with dark brown (**PHOTO F**). Finish the dirt under the overhang at the back of the carving with the clear stain over the natural wood.

8. Stab the tips of a brush lightly into brown paint and stipple it in little dots on the moss leaves. Stipple again with green and again with a slightly darker brown to create the clusters of color in a moss plant (**PHOTO G**). Lighten the green with medium yellow. Lay a very loose black on the moss so that the color soaks down to create soft shadows. Dry-brush some gentle yellow highlights.

9. Put a shadow underneath the mossy cliff itself. Then rub your thumb across the bristles of an old toothbrush dipped in a somewhat loose chocolate brown and spray the dirt under the overhang and some of the leaves (**PHOTO H**).

10. Highlight the eyelids with some white with raw umber added to it (**PHOTO I**).

Resources

A & M Wood Specialty

357 Eagle Street North
P.O. Box 32040
Cambridge, Ontario N3H 5M2
800-265-2759
www.forloversofwood.com

Heinecke Wood Products

76-27½ Ave.
Cumberland, WI 54829
715-822-8642
www.heineckewood.com

Hilcrest Carving

P.O. Box 138
3540 Marietta Ave.
Silver Spring, PA 17375
717-285-7117

Jerry-Rig USA, LLC

P.O. Box 335
Mt. Freedom, NJ 07970-0335
973-895-2818
www.jerry-rig.com

Lee Valley™ Tools Ltd.

P.O. Box 1780
Ogdensburg, NY 13669-6780
800-871-8158
www.leevalley.com

MDI Woodcarvers Supply

P.O. Box 4
Pittsfield, ME 04967
800-866-5728
www.mdiwoodcarvers.com

PJL Enterprises

720 Perry Ave. N.
Browerville, MN 56438
320-594-2811
www.carvertools.com

Ross Oar Knives

7458 Ellicott Rd.
West Falls, NY 14170
716-662-9253

Wood Carvers Supply, Inc.®

P.O. Box 7500
Englewood, FL 34295-7500
800-284-6229
www.woodcarverssupply.com

Woodcraft Supply, LLC

P.O. Box 1686
Parkersburg, WV 26102
800-225-1153
www.woodcraft.com

Index